Praise for *Do Ants Have Arseholes?*

'Childish' John Walsh, *Independent*

'This year's quirky hit' Joel Ricketts, *Guardian*

'A very funny spoof of pop-science collections' Andy Miller, *Daily Telegraph*

'Along with the Magna Carta and the Gutenberg Bible, [the British Library also] includes Wayne Rooney's autobiography and a book called *Do Ants Have Arseholes? and 101 Other Bloody Ridiculous Questions*. The MPs who in 1911 established the legal deposit principle for the five greatest libraries in the British Isles probably didn't realise the full consequences of their decision' Stuart Jeffries, *Guardian*

'We all have our theories about the reasons behind the collapse of politeness, from irresponsible parenting to vulgarity on television. I confess that a blanket of gloom descends on me when I walk into reputable bookshops and see titles such as *Is It Just Me Or Is Everything Shit?* or *Do Ants Have Arseholes?*. I can't claim that such words never pass my own lips, but I try to discourage my children from using them. I would also like to encourage them to spend time in bookshops, which ought to be treasure troves, largely free of shit and arseholes' Brian Viner, *Independent*

[He's absolutely right, Penelope. I always knew Mr Viner was a true liberal; for the good of our children bookshops ought to be largely free of – that is, containing a small quantity of – shit and arseholes. – Ed]

Also by Jon Butler & Bruno Vincent

Do Ants Have Arseholes?
Learn to Speak Mafia

DO BATS HAVE BOLLOCKS?

...and 101 more utterly stupid questions

From the popular 'Corrections & Clarfications'
page of *Old Git* magazine

JON BUTLER *and* BRUNO VINCENT

Penelope,
not again
please!

sphere

SPHERE

First published in Great Britain in 2008 by Sphere
Reprinted 2008 (four times)

A CIP catalogue record for this book
is available from the British Library.

ISBN 978-0-7515-4137-3

Typeset in Transitional by M Rules
Printed and bound in Great Britain by
Clays Ltd, St Ives plc

Papers used by Sphere are natural, renewable and recyclable
products made from wood grown in sustainable forests and certified
in accordance with the rules of the Forest Stewardship Council.

 Mixed Sources
Product group from well-managed
forests and other controlled sources
www.fsc.org Cert no. SGS-COC-004081
© 1996 Forest Stewardship Council
FSC

Sphere
An imprint of
Little, Brown Book Group
100 Victoria Embankment
London EC4Y 0DY

An Hachette Livre UK Company
www.hachettelivre.co.uk

www.littlebrown.co.uk

With many thanks to Nicola Barr, Adam Strange,
Andrew Hudson and the supreme Sphere sales team

Editor's Introduction

Welcome, *bienvenue* and *wilkommen*! As the new editor of the *Old Git*, a venerable magazine entering its seventeenth decade, I very much hope that this new volume of corrections and clarfications lives up to the high standard of the last anthology.

Following the resignation of my idiotic predecessor over the little matter of a missing work-experience student, a loaded blunderbuss and a substantial dry-cleaning bill for the office rug, it falls to me to navigate the good ship *Git* through another crude, frighteningly ill-informed collection of illiterate letters from the cretins who buy our esteemed magazine every month. [*Ha ha – Penelope, please don't type any of this up for the book; I just wrote it as a little giggle for you and me, to get us off on the right foot. I heard that the old editor's wife rubbed cayenne pepper in his sleeping mask after reading his remarks about your bosom launching a thousand ships, but I hope we shall have a more professional relationship! Here's the real introduction:*]

Welcome to the second collection of sparklingly incisive answers to burning questions that have appeared in the

Old Git magazine over the last twelve months. Regular readers will already have noticed a few changes around here: our masthead's font has switched from the calligraphic type redolent of a nineteenth-century obituary, to the smoother electric-blue font more reminiscent of a neon sign outside a jazz bar or 'pirate bookshop'. The reason? We are under new ownership. Phat Media Corp respects the values of the established brand to reflect a generation of older readers who are *getting younger*. So expect more features on tantric sex and dogging, cooler music reviews (acid jazz, electronica and hammond organ trance fusion), snow-boarding holidays, and articles that veer more towards exciting trends such as city shorts, happy slapping and designer pube trims.

To end on a more serious note: I can promise you that with change comes responsibility, and the debacle over last year's book will not be repeated. I was as appalled as so many of you were, that our publishers saw fit to print the previous volume, *Was Queen Victoria Our Greatest Monarch?*, under the absurd title *Do Ants Have Arseholes?* – a question that doesn't so much lie in the gutter looking up at the stars as do the front-crawl in a lake of excrement, looking balefully over at a rat chewing the nose off a recently deceased badger.

Of course, the legal spat which arose over the first volume's title is a matter of public record. But, with the lawyers having settled out of court (and how welcome our appointed damages were, when they arrived in the form of forty thousand copies of *Do Ants Have Arseholes?* and soaked up the effluent in our flooded basement admirably!), I am proud to present what our publisher assures us will be a stunning velum edition with marbled endpapers, entitled *Why Are Squirrels So Ineffably Cute?* Let's get this party started!

The New Editor

Has anyone ever squared the circle?

Albrecht Sprengler, Zurich

After my researches into the creation of a new colour met with muted response last year, it gives me great pride and pleasure to announce, after many months, that my attempts to find a solution to this question have paid off!

My first trials, with my daughter's plastic hula hoops and a Bunsen burner proved unfruitful, messy and hazardous. However after the fire crew had left, the garage made a more rewarding sphere of scientific endeavour than her bedroom, and I moved on to elastic bands and the four-pronged plastic pieces they put in the middle of delivery pizzas. After a mere sixteen weeks of agonising trial and error, and lots of rubber burns, I can triumphantly reveal the result:

I hope the readers and staff at the *Old Git* can benefit from this breakthrough, and that it might be the beginning of a beautiful symbiotic relationship. Perhaps a regular column giving me a chance to solve further scientific conundrums of our age?

I look forward to your response with bated breath!

SIMON SAYERS, COUNTY DURHAM

P.S. My first research task could be into what exactly bated breath is – what do you think?

[Ed note: Penelope, your new editor here. A note to Mr Sayers, I think, letting him down gently. How gratifying that our column inspires such enthusiasm, even if it is occasionally a tad wayward. By the way, this is by far the strangest office I've ever worked in. Could you ask the cleaning girl – Consuela, is it? – to scrape that 'pebbledash effect' off the wall near the door. I'm sure they're limpets. There's an unhealthy level of moisture in the whole room.]

Why is it called Custer's Last Stand, not Custer's Last Fall?

Benedict Stormish, Blasket Island

The victory of Sitting Bull's Cheyenne at the Battle of Little Bighorn is so known because General Custer, rather than the gruff macho hero of legend, was actually a sensitive aesthete who ran his battles from a silk tent on the brow of a neighbouring hill, and whose troops were represented on his battle maps by bijou trinkets of jewellery he had picked up in Southern pawn shops during the campaign. Although in stature a tall, domineering man, Custer had been a weakling child who adored French poetry and playing the flute to his pet rabbit Cécile. He had been forced into the army by his fiercely authoritative father, who would drill him for hours on end in the backyard of their ranch (ignoring the fact that Custer always kept his pristinely manicured poodle in tow, and his repeated avowal that he would rather be an interior decorator).

It was at Little Bighorn as he sat poised by his burnished chestnut harpsichord, pushing his troops around the map with an ivory toasting fork, that a stray bullet from one of the Apaches' guns thundered through the wall of the tent and shattered his last pristine piece of furniture – a mahogany music stand. Until then he had been unsure of his tactics, but a rage overcame him and, shedding his kimono and putting on his battle dress – a pink taffeta number with plumes at the hips – he led the troops in a rash and red-faced charge that resulted in his, and their, deaths. It was Custer's last fall. But then, as he would have said, it *was* his last stand . . .

JULY HI CHIO, HONG KONG

How do budget airlines get away with advertising a flight for 0.01p, only to add on lots of secret taxes just as you're about to pay?

Trevor Mental, York

I recently boarded a flight from London to Dublin, which was advertised as 'Fly for just 1p!'. The devil was in the detail, though. I remember visiting the Pyramids back in the fifties, where I paid for my wife to have a ride on a camel, only to have to pay again to get her off it, after she found herself atop a gurning dromedary and confronted by a ten-foot drop. The same principle was in force here: while the flight to Dublin might only have cost 1p, the small print of the e-ticket included eye-wateringly high extra charges for climbing the steps to the cabin, sitting down, enjoying the funny whooshing toilet, and landing. They've actually installed a coin slot on the armrests of every seat now. You spend the whole forty-five minutes feeding in ten-pence pieces – though I suppose it did take my mind off the fact the wing fell off as we were coming in to land.

CONOR O'FALLON, SLAIN

4

That's nothing, Conor; I've just heard a rumour that Budgetwings has responded to complaints about a £2 charge to check in, and a £10 charge to put your bag in the hold, and £40 tax on top of the advertised 1p fare . . . by introducing a £1 'swearbox' for every time someone says 'cock-gobbling airborne budget thieves' out loud in an airport. I reckon they're on to a winner.

MAUREEN O'HANLIHAN

[Ed note: INTERNAL ONLY – Penelope, I'm sure this will excite you, apparently as of next week we will actually be sharing offices with the Young Git, Phat Media Corp's *flagship monthly. I assumed this was a beleaguered start-up but apparently it's been thriving since the late nineties on a diet of undressed* Hollyoaks *actresses, reviews of exciting new fridge magnets, the injuries of horribly disfigured car crash/sports accident victims and bear baiting. The upshot is we received a memo from up on high which says that the* Old *and* Young Gits *are to become two different aspects of the same magazine. I never would have thought of that – shows why they get the big money, I suppose! However, because the* Young Git *sells 533,666 copies a month and we sell – well, we sell . . . well, anyway – we very much have to fall in line with them. In this spirit I've been ferreting around trying to clean out the office and have found I wasn't hanging my jacket on a coatstand but a bloody great stalagmite which has built up from the appalling dripping damp in that corner of the room. We must get Consuela on the case. Oh, and there's a funny stain in the opposite corner of the ceiling which a visitor might mistake for blood. Let's get her to scrub it out next time – or make a polite enquiry as to what's been going on at the offices upstairs!!!]*

5

Is time travel possible?

Stephen Fung, Maidstone

Indeed it is – as I was saying to my great rival, Dr Karl Beerbohm, only next Thursday. Poor Karl! I shall have my revenge for years of ridicule from you and those blasted Swedes. Even as I write this, I am preparing to go back in time, in order to balance a bucket of water on the door-frame leading to the Nobel Prize award chamber, and smear blacking powder on the eyepiece of the ceremonial telescope. Tee hee! Your smug entrance to face the world's press, on the second of December 2007, will go down in history for all the wrong reasons; and by the time this letter is printed in next month's *Old Git*, the golden bright burst of my fame will forever extinguish your achievements. See you last year, Karl!

DR JEREMY PETTING, DEPT. OF PHYSICS,
UNIVERSITY OF BANGOR, NORTH WALES

How charming of my former protégé to sport his idiocy in public in this way. Of course, as it is several weeks since his letter appeared, he will long ago have discovered that the special machinery he ordered from a mysterious PO Box in Stockholm furnished him not with the spectro-gigometer he needed, but with the parts from a child's music box and an insultingly large bill. So when he switches on the time machine, the sound that will greet his ears will not be the rushing of the space–time continuum being warped to his own infantile desires but the dulcet strains of 'The Wheels on the Bus Go Round and Round'.

Now that the (unsoaked) Nobel Prize is in my possession and my life's work secure, I am inclined to spend my days performing little pranks of the type that he has suggested. Perhaps first a visit in my own fully functioning time machine to his childhood nursery to scare the infant Petting witless with my klaxon. Then maybe a trip to the presentation hall of Bangor University on the day he is awarded his laughable doctorate, to tie his shoelaces together. Ah, the life of a Nobel Laureate is such hard work . . .

DR KARL BEERBOHM, STOCKHOLM

What is the record for suicide attempts?

Lars Smut, Gothenburg

Pretty much anything by Joy Division, but I've heard the Swedes listen to Leonard Cohen.

MR PLUM, PLUMSTEAD

[Ed note: Penelope, I rather like this Plum character. Delightfully eccentric – I can't see what my predecessor had against him.]

Is time travel possible? (Reprise)

Stephen Fung, Maidstone

O-ho! My dear Karl. I was tickled to see your letter in last month's issue; the very fact that all goes on as usual in my life tells me that your scampish prank failed. I concede that I have always been terrified of klaxons, and that on the day I was awarded my Ph.D. I pitched forward, accidentally head-butting honorary Doctor Jeanette Winterson in the process – but you knew all this; I cannot accept that you actually *caused* either of those events. How could you have done, given that I bribed your cleaning lady to jam her hat-pin in your time machine, just in case? If my calculations are correct – knowing your daily routine and chronic IBS as I do – you will just have finished your daily bowel movement before turning on the

8

machine to make your 'historic journey', only for it to skip like a dusty CD, sending you back a matter of minutes to the moment you enter the toilet again. I imagine you are stuck there now, on loop, cursing me. Perhaps I will take pity and head over to Stockholm to turn the machine off? But I seem to be very busy for the next few months, sadly.

DR JEREMY PETTING, BANGOR

How incredibly inventive of you to have jammed one of the most complex machines on earth with a *hat-pin*. You dolt. In fact, having been stuck in my ten-minute loop for, oh, about twenty minutes, I located the rogue element and pulled it out, and thereupon set about my leisurely revenge. By the time you read this, Petting, you will be able to reflect ruefully on several new memories that you will believe to have always been there: the sense of excoriating shame you felt at university when a mystery assailant took a Polaroid, while you slept, of your shrivelled and laughable gift to womankind and posted it on the Faculty of Physics noticeboard; your first horror (and concomitant paranoia) at discovering that the first conquistadores to arrive on the shores of South America found a note reading, in English, 'Jeremy Petting is a bastard', and that Venezuela's second city was named after you – Bastardo – until 1923; the fact that after you saved up for a pea-green Mini Cooper in 1978 it went missing and was discovered perched perfectly on the poop deck of the QEII. There are others, probably lost among the innumerable absurdities which you have foisted upon yourself over the course of your bumbling and

9

maladroit life. (I think the University of Bangor should know, for instance, that you only discovered that girls didn't get pregnant 'from their bottoms' in your *third week of marriage*.)

But the main reason for this letter is to announce my retirement from our little match, Jeremy. For a multitude of reasons – my bank balance is horribly low and colleagues have mentioned how much I have aged over the last six months. If only they knew I had lived six years in that time! Travelling back to Durham University to steal that car and bribe a crane driver to balance it on the *QEII*, then docked in Plymouth; recreating the Kon-Tiki expedition on my lonesome in the fifteenth century just to leave a historical insult to you – and then having to paddle *back* over the Atlantic before the Spaniards got there (and cloak myself in kelp when they passed). And of course – being a time machine and not a teleportation device – all these journeys starting from the lumpy hillock where my cottage would later be built in the 1990s. It's exhausting, and the rewards are not worth it. So I shall never again venture into the iron jaws of Karl Jr (as I had named him, in lieu of the children I might have had) to pursue scientific excellence for the purposes of pranksterdom. I shall, instead, sit, drink tea, invite friends round for 'fika', and maybe pay the occasional visit to Shakespeare's local pub, where we've got quite a chess game going.

DR KARL BEERBOHM, STOCKHOLM

I f Pinocchio was supposedly a 'real' boy made of wood, did Geppetto whittle him a wooden cock?

Ralph Coddles, Wolverhampton

Well, yes, of course he must have done; otherwise the other 'real' boys would have laughed at him in the showers at football practice after the end of the book. The notorious Parisian Obelisk Press (publishers of banned books such as Henry Miller's *Tropic of Cancer*) did actually produce a hugely controversial sequel to the Pinocchio story, *Coeur de Chair, Verge en Bois* (*Heart of Flesh, Wooden Cock*), a *Tom Jones*-like series of picaresque adventures that centre around the teenage Pinocchio in the backstreets of the Italian port of Genoa. The book remains illegal in the UK, though a full transcript can be downloaded at www.meatpuppet.org/bluefairy.net

OMAR KARIM, CAIRO

A childish question, which none the less hints at a fundamental truth that is worth examining. As with many of the best-loved fairy tales, the original story of Pinocchio was, not to put too fine a point on it, utter filth, heavily censored by Victorian translators before it ever reached the ears of English babes. I shan't descend to spelling anything out gratuitously – one can imagine the original scene of Pinocchio's 'lengthening wood' as he 'lies with' (amazing how a stray preposition can change the meaning of a sentence) the Blue Fairy, and the punishment of 'turning [that is, turning round the better to insert] his head into an ass' after the trip to the land of toys (*Il Paese dei Balocchi*) with the other boys . . . Once you know that, no fairy tale is safe. Double meanings bloom like black roses with the introduction of just a few quote marks:

'Little' Jack Horner, sat in his corner,
'Eating' some fine 'plum pie'.

Disgusting.

MALCOM BEVERLEY, BALHAM

How do polar explorers go to the toilet?

Billy Braithwaite, aged 9, London

As quickly as possible!

MR PLUM, PLUMSTEAD

2 September 1909

Dearest Marjory,

Who would be a professional polar explorer? It is with a heavy heart that I pick up this battered stub of pencil, perhaps for the last time, to write to you, oh angel of mine. Pemberton has long since stopped making sense and lies, as if grimly awaiting death, a few feet away. Baines has lost the use of his left leg, and complains of being unable to feel his face. I told him he should take off his lucky diving helmet, but he can't hear me. I fear we shall soon be forced to eat Minka, the last of our brave old dogs, and we have polished off the last of the 1899 Chablis. How can we go on? I can't help thinking that if we drink ourselves into this dreadful state in the entrance hall of the Reform Club, fully three weeks away from starting out for the Antarctic, we haven't got a hope of making the Pole.
I remain, as ever, your loving, horribly drunk
Phozzy

(Letter postmarked 3 September 1909, second class. Turned up on Tuesday.)

To answer young Master Braithwaite's question about the daily toilet of a polar explorer: the truth is every bit as prosaic and uncomfortable as you would expect. Of course you don't want a pool of frozen urine inside the tent, where it might by thawed by the fire, so you're obliged to step outside. To keep from leaving your scent in one place and attracting polar bears (and to keep moving in the cold), it is encouraged to jump around in a circle, disseminating your liquid waste in every direction on the hundred-mile-an-hour polar winds. Hence 'pissing in the wind', a phrase Shackleton brought back from his 1912 expedition.

N. COGNITO, ARCTIC CIRCLE

(PENNY! It's me, the old editor! Hope you're bearing up, old girl. I managed to pick up a few editions of the Old Git *in a bookshop in Medicine Hat, Alberta – I can see already what a pettifogging bore they've replaced me with, his pedantry and utter ignorance of the modern world. It must be unbearable for you. Anyway, the travels are as tiddly-spanking as I expected. Had a hairy moment at the Alaskan border when they refused to believe I'd hiked over the Bering Straits in nothing hardier than a pair of plimsolls and a couple of cricket pullovers. But I sorted that out and here I am in the Arctic Circle. It's a devil to get the old cigarillos sparked up, and I'm missing the World Bowls Championship as we speak, but no gain without pain, Penny! Chin up, dear girl! Oh, and of course – only print my anonymous answer above, not this note to you. There's a love.)*

Does pride come before a fall?

Toby Titting, Wollaton

I would say so, yes. I used to work with a Professor Stephen Dumughn at the Department of Sexual History in Watford, but after the professor arrogantly made fun of me for wearing stacked heels and suggested 'an office charity dwarf-toss', he was asked to move on. I have yet to see his name appear at any of the other great Sexual universities (Newcastle, Reading, Ayia Napa), and pronounce myself satisfied that his reputation is ruined.

More interesting for regular readers of the *Old Git*, is the recent discovery of papers that trash utterly the reputation of the famous adventurer Arthur 'Paddy' Staunton-Whipsthistle. 'Padso', who enjoyed such fame as an old man for having sought out the middle of nowhere in the late 1920s, was the epitome of a proud, over-educated, sneering old goat. The old fraud's foul play was uncovered in the collected diaries of his faithful cook Lacrouche, which were due to be shown on the *Antiques Roadshow* this summer. (Sadly, the producers instead decided to air remarkable footage of Michael Aspel tripping and putting his head through a five-hundred-year-old Holbein portrait, 'Lady Mary of Leicester'. Do look it up on YouTube – all that's missing is candyfloss, a laughing-policeman booth and end-of-the-pier barrel-organ music to complete the scene.) What becomes clear from Lacrouche, is that Staunton-Whipsthistle's 'hapless' manservant, Nick Blake, was actually the brains of the fearless trio. 'Lantern-jawed and deadly in unarmed combat' is Lacrouche's description of Blake, who over the course of the letters emerges as an extraordinary polymath, a veritable modern-day Erasmus who made lasting contributions to the fields of painting, navigation, philosophy, and macramé. Having found the middle of nowhere many times, Blake went on to square the circle in 1934 and in 1957 triumphantly discovered a new colour, 'International Klein Blake'. Of course, everyone knows the rest: in the winter of that year, Blake was found dead in the English channel, and his collaborator, the French artist Yves Klein, went on to make the colour famous as 'International Klein *Blue*'. Less well-known is the identity of Yves Klein's mentor, adoptive father and later lover: one Arthur 'Paddy' Staunton-Whipsthistle . . .

'LOFTY' MUNTERPOUNCE, DEPT OF SEXUAL HISTORY,

WATFORD UNIVERSITY

Corrections & Clarfications

In General Smythington-Smythe's reminiscences last week, several readers were alarmed that he claimed to have enjoyed tea with Emperor Hirohito in Kyoto in 1944, and to have performed 'Hara-kiri' afterwards. They wondered how he had come to write the column if this was accurate. The General apologises for the mistake. Working undercover for MI6 at the time, he in fact performed 'Mata-hari', i.e., sleeping with an enemy in order to gain state secrets. 'I'm not comfortable with the confession,' he writes, 'but over the course of our invaluable time together the Emperor revealed a lot of his trading passages.'

Aside from Beethoven's deafness and the blindness of Stevie Wonder and Ray Charles, are there any other examples of great musicians who've triumphed over a disability?

Brigid Donald, Istanbul

The greatest story of a musician to have lacked one sense must surely be that of the Scots-Israeli composer Yitzak MacGonagall, a mute child who was also a remarkable prodigy. He first showed his talent at eighteen months by crawling into the pub where his father was drinking, and playing 'Come home, you drunken Scottish bastard' on the piano in Morse code. Though unable to speak, he could communicate through a variety of mellifluous stylistic variations, using the full repertoire of major and minor keys to get across the most complex ideas. An estate manager for the lord of the manor who happened to be in the pub passed his name on to higher authorities and by the age of four, in 1897, he was conducting symphonies and writing string quartets in expression of love for a girl in his playgroup. Her name was Hilary, but nevertheless his love remained alive, and by his seventh birthday he was handing her into the Moscow Conservatoire for a performance of his first piano concerto.

He died at seventeen in a tragic misunderstanding when, still only able to communicate by music, he went into his local bar to ask his father for the loan of a shilling. Trying to order a ginger ale on the rickety piano, his father mistook a mazurka for a tarantella and beat him to death with a metronome. His body is embalmed at the Israeli Classical Music Foundation in Aberdeen.

ALBRECHT LE BOEUF, ISLE OF DOGS

Do bats have bollocks?

Andrew Hudson, London

Indeed they do – and then some. Some species of bat, such as the Peruvian long-eared fruitbat, are thought to have the largest testicles in the animal kingdom, proportionate to their body mass. Put it like this: if Colin Jackson had been built in the same proportions as a Peruvian long-ear, he wouldn't have done much in the 110-metre hurdles, I can tell you.

Interestingly, most zoologists have finally made the leap in logic demanded by Darwin, and now agree that bats' blindness is literally 'congenital' – that is, the product of millennia hanging upside-down, being smacked in the eyes repeatedly by a big bunch of hairy bollocks. The bigger the gonads, the blinder the bat; the blinder the bat, the more sophisticated its sonar. Big balls equals big meals, and the triumph of big-balled genes. So

18

next time you see a bat fluttering close to you in the gorgeous night air, marvel at the beauty of evolution – and duck!

MOUSY TICKLE, DARTFORD ASSOCIATION OF BAT LOVERS

It is frustrating that this myth is allowed to remain intact, owing to the wrong-headedness of the irritatingly named Mr Tickle (a name whose absurdity he lives up to in person – if we meet again, Tickle, I'll shove that feather duster you carry up your stupid bumhole). The tiny dangly appendage that hangs from a bat's crotch is in fact an external set of tonsils. The bat's *bollocks* (which the male bat does have, to answer your question, Andrew) are in fact much larger and located at the back of the creature's throat. This accounts for the strained and aggressive look they wear and the fact that they can only emit a high pitched squeak. That's the males at least – freed from this encumbrance, the female's voice is a low, dolorous baritone.

MEREDITH DE MALMO, SPITSBERGEN

[Penelope – Is it true about the people in the office upstairs? Four of them? With an axe? And all while we were sipping lattes in our fortnightly Editorial 'Content Focus' Session. How terrifying that evil lurks so close when you live in the city. It makes me pine for my time at Hedgerow Gazette. *Anyway, the chief reason for this memo is that I have just found an extraordinary note from the previous Editor that I had to share with you. It shows the sort of cad you were dealing with. Don't type it up for the column – just thought it might raise a smile.]*

My darling Iris,

You will be pleased to hear that I have finally booked a hotel room in Baden-Baden for our tryst. However, I fear I must warn you – money being short at the moment – that the Germans have a very odd system of pricing, to whit:

Doppel zimmer – 80 marks
Doppel zimmer mit shower – 100 marks
Doppel zimmer mit shower und WC – 120 marks

Would you consider 'going' in the shower, to save that extra 20 marks, do you think? There's a game girl.

What does the famous rail announcement 'Could Inspector Sands please report to platform 5' really mean?

Sally Kroop, Bayswater

This wonderfully anachronistic 'code' phrase has never been publicly explained by rail companies, but is widely believed to refer to any nameless emergency such as a fire or a dangerous spillage – especially since the platform's number changes depending on the announcement. Other favourites I've heard over the years include

'A performance of "The Ballad of Reading Gaol" will take place presently on platform 6 (translation: 'If you stand in the gutter of platform 6 and look up at the grille in the ceiling of platform 10, you can see up a woman's skirt'); 'Surf's up, beach 8' ('Someone has vomited up a kebab on platform 8'); and 'Could Deborah please spank me, lightly but firmly in the entrance hall' ('Lost Italian tourists').

TONY LYONS, WHITSTABLE

It's amazing how many people don't even think to stop and listen to the announcements when they're travelling. Do look out for this week's *Sunday Times*, however. The secret is finally out; as a journalist I thought it was my duty to take a Dictaphone into the Underground, and made a transcript of the droning mantra that buzzes away in the background to every journey. The results are genuinely surprising; a real scoop:

> Due to ongoing repairs, the Northern line, Circle line, District line, Jubilee line, Metropolitan line, Piccadilly line, Central line and Waterloo and City lines are currently suspended. All other lines – correction: the other line – is operating a good service. An excellent service, in fact. You are feeling very sleepy. You feel well, and happy. Your sex life is fulfilling. When you wake up, you will not hate Mayor Boris Johnson. He will seem taller and less like a side of beef covered in hay . . . Due to ongoing repairs, the Northern line . . .

UNADDRESSED ENVELOPE

I'm so pleased that someone else has noticed how they *tell* us what the service is like, instead of asking us! My husband works for London Underground, and I've noticed that recently, while making love, he's been talking a lot more: 'You are currently enjoying an excellent servicing' has been his mantra just before orgasm. I'm thinking of writing a letter of complaint to Mayor Johnson.

PATRICIA LOWSMITH, TOTTERIDGE & WHETSTONE

Dear Bill Oddie,

I am writing to tell you just how much I am enjoying the new series of *Springwatch*, although I don't much like the scruffy little blond boy who presents the show with you. Anyway, I'm very excited to be able to write in about the goings on that I can see from my front window: the blue tits are back, cheeky little things that they are; the squirrels have begun to emerge after their winter sleeps, and I love to see their lively, inquisitive faces as I sip my morning pint of creamy Bailey's. Oh, and Mrs Peacock from next door had an argument with her husband last night. Between you and me, Bill, it's been coming for a while. He's a shit, and she's no better than she ought to be.

Yours warmly,

VALERIE PARSNIP, BRIGHTON

Corrections & Clarfications

We would like to apologise for the errors in last month's *Old Git* column written by General Smythington-Smythe about his colonial reminiscences, where it seems we quite uncharacteristically allowed a few mistakes through. In the paragraph about his taking tea with the Sultan, the phrase 'ignorant dirty Arab scurrying away' should have read 'ignored a dirty rat scurrying away' and the epithet 'filthy bigoted bastard' was not intended to be appelled to the Saudi Minister of the Interior, but to the British Undersecretary to the Consul. We would like to apologise to the forty-seven Muslim readers who wrote in to complain, and to add, in our defence, that we didn't know you existed. *Allahu Akhbar!*

What exactly were the tabloids insinuating that Richard Gere did with a gerbil?

R. Daring, London

Rumours have circulated for years about what possible pleasure could an actor of Gere's stature derive from such a small mammal. I've never believed the reports about 'gerbilling' – the fictitious sexual practice of sitting on a restless field mouse in order to stimulate the prostate. That's about as likely as him having indulged in the even less well-known practice of 'tromboning', whereby the lips are placed on a lover's bottom while reaching round and vigorously moving up and down the musical scale. The image of the star of *An Officer and a Gentleman* attempting to conjure forth a few high, bright notes out of an erect gerbil is patently ridiculous. I cannot call to mind another member of the brass section that small. Thinking about it again, however – as I have done, all day while looking out of my office window – a large cat would be about the same size as an actual trombone—

RUFUS BARQUE, NOTTINGHAM

[Ed note: Penelope! I know we don't believe in censorship, but I do love cats. Please end the entry there.]

Thank you for cutting off the horrifying letter from Rufus Barque when you did. God alone knows what abomination it went on to describe. Here at the League for the Protection of Cats, we have done considerable research into the incidence and effects of feline sexual abuse, and have published our findings. While Mr Barque might find it casually amusing to imagine blowing up a cat's bum end while simultaneously caressing it, all our tests indicated that the cat would likely find this very disturbing and might suffer psychologically damaging repressed-memory syndrome, which could cause it to become depressed in later life. In fact the very moving story of our chief test subject, a tabby called Major Tom, has been transcribed into a shattering but ultimately uplifting 'misery memoir' with the help of his ghostwriter, a golden retriever named Ziggy. It was recently bought after a heated auction between publishers and looks likely to set the misery memoir market alight. Perhaps that will help spread the news to ordinary folk about the damage caused by treating your pets as sexual objects, and once they realise, they'll stop doing it. I know I did.

PROF. JEFFREY SCOLE, PRESIDENT, LEAGUE FOR THE
PROTECTION OF CATS

I had a cat once, but it split. Can you help?

Terry, Coventry – question remains unanswered

Whatever happened to Ronald McDonald?

Tim O'Hagan, Woldingham, Surrey

Ronald McDonald was for so long the global face of McDonald's that, just as with Michael Jackson, it is hard to call to mind just how famous McDonald himself was, back in the 1980s. Beloved of children everywhere, Ronald brought joy and grilled cow meat to the world, and no one can take that away from him.

All things must pass, of course, not least in the cut-throat, fickle world of global branding. Some say Ronald scratches a living in Vegas, marrying young runaway couples, dressed as a Chinese Elvis; others say he lives in the northern wilds of Washington State in a log cabin, living simply as a woodcutter; older now, of course – the make-up a little smudged by the elements, the bright yellow tights saggy and perhaps a little torn by brambles, the wig worn a little frizzier from the constant rain. But if the trumpeting *[should this be 'tromboning'? – Ed]* cover blurb of his soon-to-be-released novel is to be believed, the old clown has finally found some peace out there in the woods:

Ronald McDonald

The Unhappy Meal

The tears of a clown, and the pies that blind us

Paris, 1940. On the outskirts of the city, Hitler's forces lie in wait like a cat about to pounce.

Back in the present day, young Neville McCreville has little in common with the dramatic Nazi occupation of wartorn France that drew you into reading the back of this book. He is a happy boy: loved by his parents, and comfortable with his horribly disfigured face and bell-ended feet; happier, certainly, than his sly, wayward half-brother, Greville.

But things are not always as they seem in Utopia. Dark secrets lie beneath the surface of every family, tired clichés abound, and if young Neville is to become a man, he must first discover what happened to his grandmother's recipe for Special Sauce ...

BRAD CABLE, ST LOUIS

I've never really understood the proverb 'A snitch in mime serves time'. Could any of the *Old Git* readers enlighten me as to its meaning?

Kathy Parks, Nottingham

I think that Kathy Parks is talking about saving time by demonstrating industry in the short term; though I rather like the image of an East End hoodlum forcibly dressed as Marcel Marceau as punishment. Either way, the original proverb is a very useful one, time being of the essence in modern society. For my own part, I can recommend eating all of one's meals while sitting on the toilet. Gobble, chomp, plop, gobble, chomp, plop – I must be saving ten to fifteen minutes a day at the very least – and it leaves the taps free for my wife to brush her teeth.

BARNABY SLEEK, CORNWALL

[Ed note: Penelope, sorry, struggling with this newfangled Dictaphone. Thought a quiet moment on the loo might help me concentrate. Could you do me a favour? Drawing a thin veil over the questioner's awful mangling of a famous proverb, please could you not print any letters from Kathy Parks in future? She was my life partner for some time, you see; but she insists on holding against me the unfortunate misunderstanding about the meaning of 'tromboning' that occurred in Halfords' car park last summer. She had simply wanted me to play her favourite Louis Armstrong CD. It's important that I maintain an air of dignity now that those bloody modernisers down the hallway are trying to turn us

into the Young Git. *Tum ti tum – how do I turn this bloody thing off? . . . it's still making a little whir as if it's taping, don't want to be recorded whistling the theme tune to* The Archers, *very off-message . . . Ooh, flies undone . . . yellow spotting . . . must shake the end more vigorously before re-holstering . . . click]*

Does it take one to know one?

Henry Gaylord, Claygate

This popular playground taunt actually filtered down from the deep (and deeply troubling) disputes between philosophers in the nineteenth and twentieth centuries. Great thinkers trying to get past the horribly isolationist line of thought left by Descartes's 'I think, therefore I am', tried to show that outside the knowledge of our own experience we might be able to prove to ourselves that other people exist.

Heidegger and others explored this line of thought down the lonely existentialist route, but from his rooms in Cambridge, Wittgenstein, who had translated Descartes's line as 'One thinks, therefore one is', published an open letter in 1941 to other philosophers, entitled, 'Does it take one to know one?'

The only thinker who felt up to the challenge of replying was Bertrand Russell, whose published response read, simply and intriguingly, 'I know what you are, but what am I?'

ROGER DAPPELTHORPE, DUNSTABLE

It's difficult to tell whether one knows one or not. It entirely depends on whether one has met one. If one *has* met one, one is undoubtedly delighted to say that one has met one more than once.

PRINCE OF WALES, SANDRINGHAM

I knew one, once. But then again I suppose I must confess that I was one too that fateful summer, with the thunderclouds of war blooming like a dark bruise on the horizon.

I couldn't help but think back to those old, gold days of the 1930s as I drove to meet Miss Fenton. It had been many years since she and I had last spoken, and the memory of our parting weighed heavily upon me as I negotiated the twisting roads that led to the little market town of Felching. I remembered clearly the simple wonder I had felt as a boy, seeing Felching for the first time from the back seat of Father's Packard.

Of course, it would never have worked between Miss Fenton and me. Mr Brad Ferryman, an American gentleman and the new proprietor of Hartington Hall, is a kind man. He has exhorted me to take time from polishing Lord Curzon's hunting horn by the fire to seek Miss Fenton out and declare my feelings for her; but I fear our story shall forever remain one of what might have been, if I had been one and she had truly been one, too – hands touching accidentally during the evening service, and a very English inability to express strong emotions. Apart, that is, from that one time when we banged the beans out of each other in the pantry.

STEVENS THE BUTLER, HARTINGTON HALL

[Ed note: Penelope, please return the following letter to sender. I found it in a velvet-lined box under a loose board in the office. How queer!]

Dearest H,

I feel like such a bad sister for leaving it this long, but it gives me more relief than I can express to say that a great deal of prayer and patience has paid off: as of yesterday we are ensconced in this heavenly cottage, not a quarter of a mile from the picture-book village of Pittle.

Jeremy is happier than ever, rooting through the spare rooms and outhouses for rusty objects to turn into his latest exhibition, and Petunia is singing happily next to the little stream that winds through the back of our land, already chatting with a new imaginary friend.

Yet it's me who's happiest of all – I've discovered several trunks of papers in the attic that belonged to one of the cottage's previous owners. I can't tell *when* they were written exactly – they seem to have lain dormant for decades – but their author writes about a dreadful district in a huge city which was overcome with rain every day for many years and where he recorded a thousand weird and terrifying stories. The diary I found near the top of the case tells a fascinating tale from near the end of his life, when he must have been living here.

It appears that one day a girl called at his door selling him apples from his own garden. When he accused her she broke down, begging his protection. He took pity, and let her sleep in an outhouse (an *outhouse*! The brute!). In the next few entries he seems very distressed and unhappy, but it's hard to tell what's going on. Reading it in the very kitchen where it was written gives me a chilling thrill. But I've been reading all night, and the sun comes up. I must go. I'll let you know what happens!

With all my love, your devoted sister,
Clarissa

Corrections & Clarfications
We would like to apologise to the publishers Faber and Faber for our ill-thought-out decision to bill the literary event 'An Evening with Seamus Heaney' as '£10 TO HAVE A GO ON A POET'. It was a quiet afternoon in the *Old Git* office and we are under tremendous pressure from the new management to sell more tickets to our sponsored events. Everyone here wishes the Nobel Laureate all the very best, and a speedy recovery from being mobbed by nine hundred elderly readers' group members.

Is there a place on earth where, for any reason, the sun doesn't shine?

*Stephen Dumughn, Chief Height Restriction Coordinator,
Chessington World of Adventures*

Aside from the obvious fact that the sun doesn't shine on half the earth at any given time, there is an instance of a place being overwhelmed by scientifically inexplicable shadow – the city of Grantsburg in North Dakota, in 1936.

It began on a Sunday afternoon in December, just when most families had returned home from church and settled down to Sunday lunch (no doubt to be followed by wholesome apple pie in that ultra-conservative corner of America. Storm clouds gathered so dense that, within half an hour, the whole town was as black as night.

Worse, the downtown district was assailed by constant thunderstorms, lightning, hail and, two days later, a tornado that sheared off the face of an office block and tore down billboards in a half-mile path of destructive energy.

Freaked out detectives and ambulance-chasing meteorologists hunted night and day through the streets for an explanation. After a superstitious manhunt by an angry mob, on the fourth day of darkness torch-wielding crowds dragged a man forward, an unemployed shoe

factory worker named Milo Grubhorn, a shy and
sensitive fellow who had fallen into a deep depression
after his girlfriend had left him. Lightning had struck
his building forty-three times since the blackout, killing
three pensioners and a duck, and the tornado had cut
a path from outside his window to his ex-girlfriend's
address.

When lightning began to strike the crowd, they rushed
to the town hall and locked the lovelorn Grubhorn in, and
immediately dispersed. The crowd, scientists and cops took
cover while outside worse disturbances were created by the
weather. Plagues of cicadas and flapping haddocks
hammered the walls and roof; showers of rusty bicycles and
broken clocks shattered the windows. The few who were
foolish enough to venture into the town hall said
Grubhorn's intensity of unhappiness actually *sucked light
from the air*, so that it was blacker than night and hard to
see more than a grey blur even when you held a lamp in
front of your face.

Before he had been thirty hours in the battered hall, one
of the cops came up with a plan. Sixteen men lay dead in a
sea of shattered glass and bricks; the roof dipped inwards
dangerously and the bodies of penguins, grand pianos and a
printing press lay in the wreckage, all hurled at the building
in the god-like anger of the storm.

They sent runners out for the 'girlfriend', LeeAnn
Lestrange, to be brought, to try to ease the storm. She not
only refused but turned out to be a prostitute who, shown
his picture, recognised him as a client who 'was one big
no-show' and who had then cried when she left.
Eventually a massive bribe got her into the town hall.
Ducking out of a hailstorm of beef-and-onion pasties and

Greek dictionaries, the policemen retired to a ruined hotel opposite, to wait.

Hours passed, and the first signs were not good.

Snow drifted down in lazy showers and then thickened into a blizzard. Midnight came and went, and the snow drifts against the walls met those on the roof. Finally the petrified cops and fascinated meteorologists peering out saw the building disappear in a perfect pyramid of ice.

Then it stopped, and the wind stopped too. A brightening in the clouds was followed by a single ray of light that lit upon the pinnacle. Soon the empty streets were warmed by a full beam of sunshine and, within hours, the baking heat of a midsummer sun. Woken from their bomb shelters and basements, crowds gathered round as the final ice melted away and the shape of LeeAnn was discerned stepping tentatively from the wrecked doors. Warily watching the assembled crowd, she walked forward to the banks of proffered microphones and delivered her single-sentence statement: 'That boy ain't a virgin no more.'

DONALD FENELEWICZ, MYO COUNTY, OMAHA

Corrections & Clarfications
Tits. Tits tits tits. Tits, tits, tits, tits . . . tits tits tits. Tits. Tits! Tits tits tits tits tits. Tits. Tits. Tits. Tits. Tits. *Tits*. Tits tits tits.

35

'Where the sun don't shine' is American for one's 'asshole', as we all know. But why do they always say, in cop shows, 'Don't blow smoke up my ass', as meaning, 'Don't lie to me'? Where does that come from?

Peadar O'Súillebháin, Glenbeigh, Co. Kerry

Ah, what an innocent you are, Mr O'Súillebháin! (And yet, what pleasures you have deprived yourself of!) The truth is that the phrase actually originated in your own homeland, or rather in the first droves of your countrymen who made small fortunes exporting donkeys to New England ports, especially Boston, in the late eighteenth- and early-nineteenth centuries.

Naturally there was only so much feed one could pack on to ships without rendering the trip profitless. Therefore the livestock mostly arrived thin, and turned a poor profit. That was until an inventive smuggler, opium addict and pervert by the name of Dominic Lascelles, in the height of a narcotic reverie, amused his friends (and won a bet) by exhaling his pipe smoke up a donkey's backside. The following day, after he had recovered (and, one hopes, thoroughly washed his lips), he found that the donkey hadn't eaten any feed, and yet looked happy in a dopey kind of way – and, with a smoke-filled colon, it looked fatter, too.

So he disembarked at Boston with the fattest, happiest-looking donkeys and sold his entire stock within twenty-four hours to smallholders who needed sturdy, reliable and inexpensive beasts of burden. Within a year the trade was rife with this sharp practice, and the common conception of a donkey soon switched from the wily creature of Irish folklore to a dozy-eyed stupid kind of mammal. Over the course of the next fifty years or so, the meaning of the word 'ass' (as something a farmer would spend all day sitting on) fused in the American tongue with the English word 'arse', hence our current mystifying phrase.

Lascelles himself became obsessed with opium smoke ingested into the colon as a more efficient and sharply pleasurable delivery system for his drug. It didn't catch on, however; nor did the special leather-tube pipes he developed and tried to market. He ran out of money and, doped up to the gills, died in a New York slum when, keeping an almost lethal level of smoke in with a cork, he coughed violently, loosening the cork and shooting himself out of a third-storey window.

CLAUDE DEVANEY, MUSEUM OF CORK USAGES,
ODESSA, TEXAS

Corrections & Clarfications
Dear tits. Please accept our tits for the fact that the 'auto-replace' function was tits again in last month's special feature on tits. Penny, can we get some tits over here? Tits.

Is it possible to make a mountain out of a molehill?

Jill Trent, Spillane, N.J.

Actually on the many miniature sets used for the *Lord of the Rings* trilogy, just this was done. This is admitted on the thirty-four-disc Ultra-Ultimate Final Collector's Edition box set, which New Live Studios released due to 'popular demand' six months after the twenty-two-disc Limited Edition Special Director's Cut box set. On the *eighth* commentary track (or 'yak track'), where the film is discussed by the wardrobe assistants, gaffers and best boys (the *ninth* audio track features all the midgets used on set – not the performers, just the ones who held ladders and fixed fiddly machinery), it is revealed that many of the mountain ranges in the trilogy are not carefully rendered CGI but rows of molehills filmed in extreme close-up. A team of specially trained, highly paid moles were kept on set to dig through specific types of soil to create the different aesthetics needed. Mount Doom was made in this way, regarded as the masterwork of Big Billy, a burly, heavy-set mole who burrowed through cooling tar and used coffee grounds to create the desired effect. Other secrets from the meticulously intricate miniatures work on the film emerge from the commentary: apparently the majestic sequence where the overflowing river floods the fires of Orthanc was inspired by a mammoth drinking session in which Elijah Wood threw up over a large table covered with drinks and smouldering ashtrays.

NIAMH SHEPSWORTH, NOTTS

Surely there can be no better example of a mountain being made from a molehill than the argument that broke out in 1898 between an Austrian patent clerk and his wife over the washing up. She was an obsessional clean-freak called Mileva who, instead of drying one of the dishes she was handed, offered it back to her husband insisting that he 'wash it properly'.

'That is proper!' he shouted. 'What am I hearing?'

She is supposed to have pointed to an infinitesimal speck of dirt remaining on the plate's rim.

'That? I scrubbed it for thirty seconds! It's the cleanest bit of dirt in the universe! And it's as small as an atom!'

The argument escalated until the clerk shouted that, if she wanted him to split the atom, then by all means, that was what he would do. Gathering his hat and coat he stormed out to the local library, the only place where the impecunious man wouldn't have to buy something to sit down. You've already guessed that the man's name was Albert Einstein, but you probably didn't know that he had no interest in physics until this moment. In fact, it was his fury at his wife's intransigence that drove him to the science section to start swotting up, and, when he returned home and found her in a permanent sulk, the library became a habit that he resorted to each evening and all day at the weekends. That – and the girl at the counter was very pretty. So he was driven to sheepishly ordering up more and more esoteric books on physics until to his astonishment he discovered he had the most natural knack for the subject of anyone in the entire world.

Women are multi-taskers; men are obsessives. After seven years, so engrossed was he in the deep sums of particle physics and so in love with Enid, the pretty and tantalisingly single librarian, that he decided to compose the most complex equation ever known to man. His general theory of relativity came from a molehill and became the mountain whose shadow dominated the twentieth century and hangs over us still. But the Scots émigré Enid McCarthy remained stolidly unimpressed with his masterpiece, $E=mc^2$, which he considered a scientific poem to her – distraught, the fanatically dapper Einstein let his appearance go until he looked like an electrocuted tramp. McCarthy, meanwhile, married an Italian futurist poet who wrote her verses about atomic physics. She didn't understand them either, but he was rich.

KAREN PUBRIS, OTTAWA

Can any of those WWF guys really wrestle? Or are they as they seem, a bunch of butch but actually rather effeminate actors?

Jamie Wicks, Le Havre

We all secretly know the answer to this – they're pussycats. It is axiomatic that the changing rooms in arenas at WWF performances, or 'matches', are to wrestling what the ladies' changing rooms at Wimbledon are to tennis – only more shrill. Take the 'Death Match' in

March last year at Pasadena between Project X, the Gravedigger and TNT. A mouse ran into the ring halfway through and the wrestlers broke into a frenzy of high-pitched screaming and began running in panicked circles, flapping their hands. Two of them climbed cornerposts and refused to come down until the creature had been shooed away by a fat black woman with a broom. The third, TNT, rampaged into the audience, and was only calmed by the promise of a pedicure.

MARY SICKNOTE, CASTLEVILLE, MISSOURI

I actually lived with one of these guys on Venice Beach in the early nineties. We were both trying to make it as actors in Hollywood at the time. I subsidised myself working as a waiter, while my roommate Algernon worked as a WWF wrestler called WMD.

Like many 'wrestlers' he came from the performing arts, having successfully completed a few seasons in Soho theatres in New York (where his Ophelia garnered much praise), although his original training was in ballet. Whenever he heard he had failed an audition he would cry, 'O that this too, too sullied flesh would melt, thaw and resolve itself into a dew!' and perform the dance of the sugar plum fairy around our living room. Like many of us, he eventually gave up on his dream, crushed by rejection (the closest he ever got was as a stand-in for Samuel L. Jackson's hairdo in a straight-to-video thriller), and the last I heard of him he was teaching an embroidery class in Oakland.

JIMMY BUCK, SAN DIEGO

41

Dear Marjory,

What exhaustion, what Olympian endurance has brought us to this unhappy pass — what misery! what physical duress! what little reward for the courage that only true Englishmen on a hopeless quest could show! O!

But let me relate my tale from the start. Three days of ice-cold trudge through impenetrable fog showed us not a single marker to tell us how far — if anywhere — we had progressed on our trek. That Apsley Cherry-Garrard chap had given up and gone home days past, lily-flower that he is (missing the ballet, perhaps, or pining for the warmth of his butler, a rugged botanist fallen on hard times, with whom I am convinced he shares his bed).

And then we saw it. Looming gaunt and majestic in the swirling mist, the ancient, wind-reddened face of the largest of walking beasts, resting forward on its haunches and exuding a hissing noise as of a ten-tonne cobra readying to strike.

We reacted as one. I charged with my harpoon and pierced the tough hide of its face with a hideous war cry. Baines threw one of our lanterns against its side, sheathing it in flame, and Pemberton hollered disorientating shamanistic incantations and spiked it up the jacksie with a lacrosse stick. The struggle lasted some minutes and amid our screams the groaning of the red-faced beast grew more intense until, having dragged us fifty yards along the featureless scree, an impertinent little man stuck his face from the creature's side and piped that we could make all the fuss we liked but that the fare from Trafalgar Square to the Reform Club was still a penny.

We were exhausted and, I confess, beaten, so we trooped aboard only to discover we didn't have a farthing between us. Thus we sit ignominiously housed in the local gaol! I could not imagine such privations being visited upon the basest savage in the heart of the Congo, nor the loneliest forlorn traveller in Antarctica. Only seven servants have been allowed to join us, and the doors were not wide enough to admit the picnic hamper! We want only for three crowns' bail, which I would reluctantly sue that you send, dearest Marjory, love of my life, by postal order? The future of our great expedition depends on it, and Pemberton's hysteria will not abate until we are guaranteed our freedom, I am sure.

Your ever-loving,

Phozzy

(Letter postmarked 18 December 1909, second class. Arrived Thursday.)

If a tree crashes in a forest and no one is there to hear it, can we say for sure whether the fallen tree is the fault of my cheating scumbag husband Leonard? I certainly think so.

Deborah Mews, Slough

Dear Deborah,

Unacquainted as I'm not, I mean as I am, with your husband, I do however sympathise with your plight. He does come across as a most unscrupulous individual. My house stands but three metres from the edge of the cliff here in North Devon, the rockface being eaten away at an ever-increasing rate thanks in part to the effects of global worming (a grotesque-sounding process I do not entirely understand) and your husband Leonard! He must be stopped!

GOLDIE RINSE, NORTH DEVON

Dear Mrs Mews,

I have to chime in with Goldie on this one. As I drove home from Tesco the other day I lost concentration for a moment and pranged my pristine 1936 Honda Civic against a 'Danger: Collapsed Bridge' sign after careering over a sleeping policeman. As the ambulance carted the drunken officer's corpse away and the recovery men winched my car I got the distinct sense that this was your husband's fault. Although I have never met you, and had never heard your name until seeing it in the August issue, I join you in condemnation of this 'scumbag' (perfect word for the cad!) Leonard. A public apology and financial reparations to the policeman's family must surely follow.

MAUREEN HAWSER, HAMPSTEAD

[Ed note: Penelope, no doubt Mr Mews regrets his actions. Yet, I don't feel comfortable with what seems to be a bit of a

44

'scapegoating' exercise. Let's not allow this to continue. By the way, valued colleague, I hate a stuffy atmosphere in the workplace, and I like people to speak their minds. Even so, I hope you can see that I felt a little uncomfortable welcoming our new CEO into the 'boardroom' (fine name for a broom cupboard that smells like a urinal) the other day when you came in to deliver his cup of decaf and plonked it in front of him with the words, 'There you go, matey-chops, get your laughing gear around that little bad boy.' Old-fashioned good manners do have their place occasionally, you know!]

If Waterloo is in Belgium, why is it made up of two English words?

Boris Cheesed, Wapping

The place name 'Waterloo' is actually thought to be of Dutch origin, from the word 'water', meaning 'water', and 'lo', which is an archaic Dutch word for a forest. Since the embarrassing annihilation of the French army at Waterloo in 1815, however, the word's meaning has subtly changed. Gone are the connotations of leafy glades, perhaps a gentle brook babbling in dappled sunlight; the *American Heritage Dictionary* defines the noun 'waterloo' as meaning 'a final, crushing defeat' (for the French), while Oxford's lexicographers instead term it 'a decisive defeat, or failure' (on the part of the French). I can finally set the record straight, however, that these humiliating historical connotations had no bearing on the decision of our government to welcome our Gallic cousins travelling to London by Eurostar, into Waterloo Station. None the less, the fact that this has now been changed to King's Cross St Pancras is lily-livered political correctness gone mad!

THE RIGHT HONOURABLE GILES SMELLING,
TORY MP FOR DOVER 1984–1997

Ah, Smelling, *mon pauvre idiot*. It has taken many year of lobbying to change this, and for the first time in fifteen year, the French people we can arrive in Britain without what I believe you call 'the thumb up the nose'. This is all in the past. But I am delighted to use this opportunity to announce that, with immediate effect, Eurostar trains will no longer arrive in the *Gare du Nord* in Paris, but instead in the newly refurbished *Retraite de Dunkirque Internationale*.

JACQUES LECROUTON, DEPT OF TRANSPORT, PARIS

I believe that a nearby town, Breughlin, gave the name to the area when rumours spread of Wellington's famous mockery of Napoleon. Although a career soldier and future prime minister of Great Britain two times over, Wellington had a great fondness for tomfoolery and 'low comedy' and, although he had never met the French Emperor, he revelled in the stories he heard about the 'maniac imp', as he called him. During the revolutionary wars, after a particularly rousing evening with his colonels and several bottles of claret, he would cavort through the rooms of the overseas headquarters cackling and screaming in a wild French accent, gurning, groaning, limping and performing what sound to us now like approximations of the Monty Python Ministry of Funny Walks, in a brilliant impersonation of a mad man. His colonels found this hilarious, and on the morning of the great battle he took his much-loved impression on to the parade ground before the assembled troops, improving morale hugely with the ridicule he poured on the Gallic leader, most of all in his broken English taunt that (making fun of the French habit of using sand toilets) we would 'waterloo all over zem!'

Only one of the generals on the field, General Thorndike (also known as Lord Droughton, who went on to become a force in the Lords for the recognition of sexually transmitted diseases), could remember the time in 1803 when Wellington, blind drunk, had stumbled into the Admiralty and unwittingly revealed that he had never been able to tell the difference between Napoleon and Nelson. Seeing who he thought was the Continental Emperor quaffing a victory gin at the bar, Wellington surrendered the forces of Great Britain and burst into tears, curling up into a ball. It seems that Thorndike got him away and into a Hackney carriage in time, before Nelson spotted the commotion – which happened on his blind side.

CECILY FLUKE, CRICKLEWOOD

47

Dear Bill Oddie,
I can't stop, Bill – like you with your little utility flak jacket,
I'm always ready for anything, and this morning Gerald
shouted at me that he wanted 'to see some damn beaver
for real, for a change' before storming out. Imagine that,
Bill: a beaver dam here in Brighton! Oh, I'm so happy;
Gerald is usually so curmudgeonly about my nature
watches, after I nursed that rabid, lame badger back to
health in our en suite toilet. I'm not sure where Gerald has
gone to see the beavers, but he spends such a lot of time in
the A37 lay-by with friends from all over town, so perhaps I
will start looking for him there? Anyway, keep up the good
work, Bill; I've got my flask of Bailey's, my binoculars and
an old electric cattle-prod I found in Gerald's funny
medieval attic conversion. Beavers, here I come!

VALERIE PARSNIP, BRIGHTON

W hy is it that even now, after years of
ridicule, there are still so many spelling
mistakes in the *Guardian*?

Larry Blues, Hemel Hempstead

Equal opportunities. The *Guardian* are not only
considerate of the environment and of the less privileged in
the world in the stories they publish, but also in the people

they hire. I had always desperately wanted to be a proofreader but my dyslexia had been an immovable obstacle until I met the wonderful staff at the *Guardian*. I've now been there nearly thirty years, and while it takes me three times the hours it would take anyone else and the occasional mistake slips through, they are very understanding. I really love this job, which I never thought I could do – trying to make sure I correctly spell my nearly rude-sounding surname would be effort enough for most dyslexics!

BEVERLY TWAT, GLOUCESTERSHIRE

[Ed note: Thank God the Old Git *does not suffer from this affliction! This question takes me back to my salad days at* Total Carp *magazine. Penelope, best get a letter off to Ms Twat, apologising for this uncharacteristic error, and get Barney to write a correction. If that's her name, I can't see what she's worried about. I didn't know this word before: apparently it means vagina. What a fuss over such a natural thing! By the way, I can't say I'm entirely happy about the noise that comes out of the* Young Git *office. 'Music' it may be, it sounds like the nightmare of a stroke victim to me. And the editor, that chap called Marc with the haircut I don't understand, brings ridiculous complaints to me that someone's been 'pissing in their milk'. Heaven knows what that's a euphemism for – I try to be understanding but I can't deny I find the man disingenuous at best and rather odious in general. Oh – and to Consuela: yes, please cleanse the high window of its near-tentacled mould, and try to eradicate whatever it is living under the floor tiles. Whenever I step on it there is a squeak and it slithers under the desk.]*

Corrections & Clarfications

We would like to apologise for the accidental misspelling of Ms Twat's name in the above-printed letter. Of course we realise that her name is, in fact, Twat. Our mistake is, as our legal department suggests we point out, in no way intentional or mocking of either her name or her linguistic disability.

We would also like to apologise for any misunderstanding created by a certain sentence in the latest instalment of Gen. Smythington-Smythe's reminiscences. In last week's episode, where he described meeting a South African general in the Johannesburg Hilton in 1960, in the sentence, 'I recognised the fat racist bastard by the, blind bilious hatred in his eyes and the bloated set of his face', the comma should have fallen after the 'blind', and not the 'the', as printed.

I s it in the job description of an estate agent that they be a smug bastard?

Jenny Frusome, Moorgate

Legally, it is forbidden for employers to stipulate that applicants for any job cleave to any specific personality traits. Yet certain types do graduate towards certain jobs, it's true. So where an advert for a job as an estate agent might as well say, 'Barefaced liars and shallow frauds only need apply', one for a job in television might read, 'Glib shit who thinks he's three times as clever as he is would be ideal', or one for a teaching position (contrary to the current posters showing bright smiling teachers surrounded by bright smiling pupils), 'FUCKING MUG'.

CLEA LASSEY, EX-ESTATE AGENT, EX-TV RESEARCHER,
EX-TEACHER, HOVE

God, I hate estate agents. I get my own back every week in my electrical goods store, though; if I find out that a browsing customer works in real estate, I only give them five minutes to look at the new television from one angle (the back), 'forget' the price of any hidden insurance costs and then, as they leave the building, take the TV back forcibly, pretending that a new buyer has just offered more money for it. It's petty of me, I know, but tremendous fun.

JANE CRAMB, LONDON

Dear Bill Oddie,
I just wanted to let you know that this morning I pulled aside the curtains and caught sight of movement through the new buds of the beautiful silver birch at the end of our garden. I immediately raced to get my binoculars, as any

51

good *Springwatch*-watcher should. In the dark corner by my husband Gerald's potting shed, where there is a small hole in the fence through to Mrs Peacock's garden next door, I saw a man's juddering bare bottom. I think it might have been Gerald's. Also, the daffodils are out. Spring has sprung!

Warmest regards,
VALERIE PARSNIP, BRIGHTON

Dear Mrs Parsnip,
We value all of our readers' contributions here at the *Old Git* and consider ourselves to be an informal, friendly sort of publication. I'm sorry that we found your last letter unprintable, but I suggest you send these messages to your husband, or the police, or Bill Oddie, who does not work here. Yet. In the meantime I wish you a happy Christmas (who cares that it's only May!) and productive gardening, and look forward to further correspondence from you that is not themed around the alleged goings on, fascinating as they are, in Brighton.
Yours, the new Editor

[Ed note: Penelope, I can't deny that I felt a moment's annoyance when I saw this letter printed in the column, alongside the one I had deemed 'unprintable'. That is one way of communicating with Mrs Parsnip, I admit (if that is her real name. I have only known one man named after a vegetable, a Mr Swede, and he made off with some traveller's cheques of mine adding up to nearly twenty pounds, so perhaps I am ill-disposed), but I feel a kinder

one would be to write to her direct. And a friendly request: next time I accidentally leave my flies undone, tell me. This morning's board meeting was a thoroughly shaming experience. My first OHP slide was a catastrophe – a huge bobbing silhouette appeared which was familiar to me but not to the rest of the audience, and lent an unwelcome Freudian air to my analysis of the peaks and troughs of our advertising revenue. Please try to pay attention, Penelope.]

Why do people say, 'there's nothing worse than . . .' when describing really innocuous things?

Horace Mantivore, Brent Cross

I have always wondered this – in fact it was a phrase used often by my late wife. In the course of a given day she might say, 'Ooh, there's nothing worse than catching your finger in a drawer' or 'There's nothing worse than a cold cup of tea'. This was back in the mid-forties at the beginning of our marriage, when we'd just set up home in Cumberland and when fresh revelations of the unimaginable horrors of the Holocaust featured in every edition of the newspaper. It was a habit that continued through the fifties and sixties when, in order to prevent myself remarking upon her (by now mildly irritating) verbal tic, I began to keep a diary of its use.

During the two weeks of the Cuban Missile Crisis, when common folk of the world looked up at a grey sky expecting it to crack with annihilating thunder, I recorded that in her opinion there was nothing worse than finding that you'd run out of loo paper while you were on the toilet, than finding a spot of shell in a fried egg, or dropping a button which rolled under the settee just beyond your reach.

The diary filled out to three volumes. On 11 September 2001, forty minutes after the news broke, she complained that there was 'nothing worse than a cancelled game of tennis'. Two years later, within an hour of hearing of her beloved brother Rodney's death, I heard her in the bedroom insisting nothing could be so bad as a counterpane that wouldn't tuck in. Then, last week, as she took her Valentine's card from me, she repeated the famous mantra in reference to a bird's dropping on our freshly washed Renault's windscreen.

I don't quite know what happened. I'm pretty sure I wanted to know the answer, but then again, as my lawyer suggests, maybe I was temporarily insane. I picked up the breadknife and stuck it in her neck and, as she fell to the floor, asked earnestly and desperately, 'Is it worse than that? Is it?'

Perhaps I shouldn't have chosen her neck, because she couldn't speak. Now I'll never know.

LEOPOLD FURTHER, MAIDSTONE POLICE STATION

H as anybody seen my cat, Jasper? He's big
and white and fluffy and I haven't seen him
for a week. Oh!

Mrs Dudge, Kettering

Mrs Dudge, prepare yourself for the worst. I fear the cat
may have fallen prey to 'catnappers' who will try to extort
money from you. But harden yourself to the following
sentence. These heartless brutes almost always kill the
cat and don't return it. If this turns out to be the case
please call our helpline or visit our website to hear about
support groups for those who've been through similar
tragedies. If the body is recovered you can always have
him stuffed, remember, and we can put you in touch with

a brilliant taxidermist. The results are remarkably lifelike, and you can ignore scaremongering about cats still being alive when cut open, it's very rare, and has only happened to one of my cats once. Poor Mulligatawny, he was always so hard to wake up, it was only a matter of time before I assumed the worst. But he looks great on top of the china cabinet, claws splayed and a fearsome expression of animal defiance on his face. Some visitors think it is one of agonising pain, but I don't see it, myself.

PROF. JEFFREY SCOLE, PRESIDENT, LEAGUE FOR THE
PROTECTION OF CATS.

We have allowed enough time for the cranks to show themselves, but in fact *we* hold Jasper. The enclosed photo of him on a deck chair reading today's newspaper proves this. Do not try to contact us. We will make our demands through this column.

ANONYMOUS

[Ed note: HOW HORRIFYING! Must we print this, Penelope? I suppose it would be irresponsible not to. But to be caught up in such a thing! It puts me in mind of the time I had to choose between keeping my pet worm and going fishing with my father, with whom my therapist says I still have complex issues. (But then she disagrees with my use of the word 'whom'. What does she know?) How the taste of the trout we caught died in my throat. Baked, as it was, with butter and toasted almonds, and served with steamed broc and boiled pots. Bitter, bitter, that moral compromise. And

Baked Alaska to follow. ANYWAY! We must regrettably follow the story!]

Don't believe Mrs Dudge. We live over at number 38, and she's been swanning around all week in Lidl with a lovely new hat that just *happens* to be big and white and fluffy. Don't give her your sympathy, fellow readers!

SARAH BLAKE, KETTERING

Why do footballers talk about giving 110 per cent? Are they innumerate?

A. S. Byatt, Wolverhampton

On the contrary – in fact footballers who speak this way are talking in simple economics. With the rise of sporting agents most players these days are forced to perform to 110 per cent at least – although 120 per cent is becoming more common – just to make ends meet. And even the most celebrated and well-paid player can struggle towards the end of their careers, if they have ex-wives to support and alimony to pay. The next time you see a player on the pitchside at the end of a game saying he's given 140 per cent or 150 per cent, don't pity his poor skill with numbers. He's just running the sums over and over in his mind, hoping they'll add up.

JAMIE SNOOP, CROUCH END

I must say, as a games teacher I strenuously ask that the FA take it upon itself to outlaw this ridiculous phrase. Having seen every one of his heroes on *Match of the Day* 'giving 110 per cent', one of my poor charges, Blenkinsop, mistakenly gave 143 per cent – leaving just a pair of empty, smoking football boots and a trace of yellow oil, somewhat reminiscent of the scene of spontaneous combustion from Dickens's *Bleak House*. Competitive sports are now banned at Haberdashers' College, and any boy seen to be giving more than 90 per cent – even in an innocuous game of Ludo or dominoes – is immediately hosed down and sent home without his lunch.

BRIAN TEMPLETON, SOUTH LONDON

How did a name like Horatio Hornblower get past the censors?

Benet Donald, Istanbul

Ah! Mr Donald unwittingly unlocks a Pandora's Box of literary filth with this question! C. S. Forester's not alone – other writers have revelled in creating filthy names ever since literature began – indeed, the Lady Chatterley obscenity trial marked a sad end to such underhand literary pranks. Hamlet's words to Ophelia, 'Do you think I meant country matters?' were positively prim compared to those of some of his successors.

Beatrix Potter's creation Mrs Tiggywinkle was in fact named after an especially hard-to-perform but rewarding method of masturbation that she had been taught by her cousin among the cabbage rows behind her house; Virginia Woolf's Mrs Dalloway is the name of a form of feminine pleasure, named after the gym mistress who scandalously propagated it, popular in boarding schools at the time (the technique has passed out of knowledge, but apparently involved doing a handstand and tucking your feet behind your ears); the original title of *The Lord of the Rings* was singular, a double-pun on Sauron's all-powerful trinket and Frodo's complete mastery of Samwise in the back alleys of the Shire (and Henry James rather broke cover with his creation Fanny Assingham in *The Golden Bowl*).

But as for Horatio Hornblower (and what does Horatio rhyme with?), this was a compromise reached after Forester's first list of names were all thrown out by the publishers – they included Shitkicker, Arselicker, Cocksnorter and Jeremy Clarkson.

H. H. UNSELF & D. DUMBLE, BROCKHAMPTON

If you eat poo, do you poo food?

John Wordsworth, Stoke Newington

Good lord, no – your solid waste contains as many of the indigestible and toxic contents of your food as your body can filter out. It's therefore chronically and dangerously poisonous. As I discovered after a not-in-the-least funny trick played on me by my 'time travelling' colleague Karl Beerbohm at the Physics department's bash to celebrate my fortieth last year. I can no longer even look at chocolate mousse.

DR JEREMY PETTING, UNIVERSITY OF BANGOR

Surely, since pigs eat their own poo, and they poo poo, but they eat poo, they poo food? And then, having pood food, they eat food and poo poo, but eat poo and poo food at the same time, over and over? Does anyone else's head hurt?

MILO SVELIC, BRNO, CZECH REPUBLIC

[Ed note: Penelope, let's keep a little closer handle on the letters we publish, shall we? I can't help feeling the above is a little below the standard our readership expect (or perhaps I overestimate them! Ha ha!). By the way, how do you feel about this Young Git-*branded merchandise we keep being given? I find these baggy jeans most uncomfortable and, I fear, they expose the band of my lower-spine-*

supporting prescription briefs. And this 'record bag' is no good at all – it rubs on my collar bone and is quite the wrong size for my old 78s. A total misnomer. Are you finding the same?]

Are the countless folk tales of the bibles and cigarette cases stopping bullets in the First and Second World Wars true? Are guns that weak, or those items so strong?

Billie Bew, Hoxton

Billie doesn't seem to realise that bibles are specifically tested against this criterion before they're printed. Why do you think there are so many different types and sizes of the Good Book? It's too long a list to give in full but, for instance, the King James small-print version can stop a .22 bullet; the standard Good News Bible is good for a snub-nose .38, and there is a leather slipcased edition of the hardback Gideon's bible that can stop a round from a .44 Magnum.

You might wonder how this all came to be known – actually it was from the lawless days of priest-hunting in Mexico (as described by Graham Greene in *The Power and the Glory*), where outlawed priests could be shot on sight. Therefore they quickly learned which publishers could supply the most protective publication.

I researched this for an article I wrote in *The Tablet* a few years ago, and since then, in these times of fanaticism and religious intolerance, I always carry a big print children's illustrated bible clutched to my chest. Except when I'm saying mass on Sundays – and then I keep a spare Collins Gem New Testament Bible in an ankle holster under my quick-release Velcro cassock.

FR LOUIS DARRANT (EX-SAS), MALDON, ESSEX

I was interested to read how such famous wartime clichés – bibles stopping a bullet and whatnot – are often just an inverted version of the truth. Funnily enough, our annual game of footy one Christmas day was interrupted by four years of dogged trench warfare between the major industrial European powers. I was a bit hacked off, to be honest; I'd just been awarded a clear penalty, only to have my horse shot from under me by the Austro-Hungarian Empire. So much for the spirit of Christmas, Mr Boche!

PRIVATE BARNEY STOKES, PIDDLINGTON FC BATTALION

Faithful worshippers out there may find this hard to stomach (and, yes, of course the scriptures are essential well-springs and pillars of every world religion), but in fact men of whatever cloth have only ever carried individual copies of their creeds, or holy books, as a ready form of defence (or attack). Not Buddhist monks, though: so long as they're getting it right, the monks should be at peace with the universe and happy in the knowledge that they do not need to repel an attack as they will be reborn as something else – if they've any luck, something that's allowed to get laid.

BRUCE T. BRAILLE, BRAINTREE

I've always wondered if the *Old Git* readers could answer Steve Wright's brilliant question: if toast always falls butter side down, and cats always land on their feet, what happens if you tie buttered toast to a cat's back and drop it from a tall building?

Eugene Mantickle, Golders Green

This is an intriguing question, which has been studied in great depth by departments of physics the world over in an effort to isolate the very nature of chance or luck, or to prove or disprove its existence.

But I have grave doubts about the questioner here. It is not the discomfort to the animal of having buttered toast tied to its back that I object to, nor the humiliation of dropping it in public while wearing this ridiculous food costume. No, it is the *tallness* of the building stipulated by Mr Mantickle that causes me unease. Would a six-foot fence not do? Even aside from the manifest and horrible cruelty to felines, picking a multi-storey car park (for instance) for your purpose must be scientifically suspect as well. Surely, should the building be taller than, say, four or five storeys, other factors come into consideration – high winds and low flying aircraft, to name but two. I speak from bitter experience, and beg Mr Mantickle not to try this at home!

PROF. JEFFREY SCOLE, PRESIDENT, LEAGUE FOR THE
PROTECTION OF CATS

Too late, I realised the wisdom of Prof. Scole's advice before it had the chance to be printed. My obsession had been growing all my life, from dropping a frog tied to a crouton from the bridge over the pond when a child, to the drunken fresher-week fun of throwing a ferret taped to a croissant (buttered, they were always buttered) from the Hammersmith flyover. Cats and bread was the next logical step. Poor Mr Cuddles! Now but a hastily mopped smear on the pavement in front of the Unilever Building. I know it now – I need help. Please, somebody stop me, before I graduate to my projected masterwork: a horse strapped to the world's biggest French loaf, cast from the observation deck of the Eiffel Tower. *Sacre bleu!*

EUGENE MANTICKLE, GOLDERS GREEN

[Ed note: Penelope, I have to confess to some alarm at reading this. When I took over the job, I hoped our average reader was something like my brother-in-law Barnabus: a quiet respectable gent who would tackle the Old Git's

Satanic Sudoku™ page before settling down to a light lunch
of cheese and crackers. But consider my expectations revised
considerably downwards – I see now the readership is not to
be flattered and pleased but feared and shunned. By the way,
from the lump of resin next to your roll-up cigarettes on your
desk I see you're a fellow violinist. Remind me to lend you my
Paganini records.]

Dear Bill Oddie,

How are you? How marvellous it is to be able to share the changing of the seasons with you and your lovely fat face. The sap is rising, Bill, and the wild, spurting growth of early summer is in sight! The cats are at it like knives on the back garden, and our dog, Clarence – as lovely a bichon-frise as you ever laid eyes on, all crisp white curls and curious expression – would fuck a pigeon lately, he's so wound up. Pardon my French, Bill!

What else? Well, Gerald has been visiting Mrs Peacock next door much less frequently since the cattle-prod incident at the beaver watch, and I think that, finally, we're on the right track, Bill. I couldn't have got here without your support, and your friendly, furry ears. I love you, Bill, but I am a married woman and Gerald is really putting some effort into his appearance, trying to win my affections back. He has taken to wearing a delightful toy bear in the back pocket of his blue jeans, and has cultivated a magnificent bushy moustache to match that of his new friends, Emile and Maurice. Oh Bill, I'm so, so happy.

VALERIE PARSNIP, BRIGHTON

Corrections & Clarfications

We should like to apologise wholeheartedly to fresh-faced newlyweds Mr and Mrs Matthew Cassie, who won last month's competition to 'Honeymoon in an authentic period Parisian guesthouse' at the *Old Git*'s expense. We had no idea that the hotel's unspecified period was in fact that of the fourteenth century, when the city of romance was riddled with the Black Death and feral gangs of bandits roamed the streets looking for an easy mark; and we hope that Sarah and Matthew will accept a handsome ten-pound book token by way of recompense for their ordeal.

[Hey Molly, take this down, yeah? Thanks, mate. Don't forward it outside the Young Git *office, though: 'Hey Guys, the new editor of the* Young Git *here, but you can call me Marc with a "c", yeah? So listen, I don't know what it means, but since we moved into the same corridor as the* Old Git, *someone's been replacing my lunchbox in the fridge with a parcel of shit. All it says on the parcel is "We don't want you here, you young git". Does anyone know who sent it? I mean, I'm a reasonable guy, so I'm happy to listen if anyone's got a grudge? Peace, Marc.']*

Do giraffes sleep standing up?

Randolph Trute, Lynchburg, Virginia

That giraffes sleep standing up is a hoary old myth first found in Aristotle's *De incessu Animalium*, and laid to rest definitively as long ago as the seventeenth century in Sir Thomas Browne's magisterial *Pseudodoxia Epidemica*. Browne concedes that, in order to sleep, the giraffe must by necessity *'drapeth its great Neck oer a nearby tree and slowly lowereth its legs till Earth were reached'*, before uncurling its neck and lying down, but pooh-poohs the notion that it might be impossible for the giraffe to lie down at all. Many 'old, gray-headed' myths are similarly discounted by Browne's cool-headed reasoning: that elephants have no joints, for instance (*'This absurdity is seconded with another, that being unable to lie down, it sleepeth against a Tree; which, the Hunters observing, do saw it almost asunder; whereon the Beast relying, by the fall of the Tree, falls also down itself, and is able to rise no more.'*); but he also comes up with some fascinating proofs: *'That elephants are afeard of Mice is True, for the latter by necessity do seek out darkened holes, the finding of which, it might be understood, must surely causeth much distress and Trumpeting for the owner of such holes.'* A man well ahead of his time.

DR ROB BRITTAIN, INSTITUTE OF MAMMALIAN
SLEEP STUDIES, BERWICK

Quite the opposite. In fact giraffes sleep *upside down*, digging holes with their hooves to stick their heads into. They can be seen in the early African dawn with all four feet sticking up, towards the sky. In fact we get the term 'rubbernecking' from the numbers of safari-makers who pay top dollar to elite scouts so they can witness this up close. They then take videos of each other pushing the giraffes' bodies back and forth to great comic effect, as the animals bounce on their super-resistant and rubber-like neck muscles. That is, until the giraffes wake up, which happens quite quickly, when they can be pretty pissed off, and have been known to angrily hoof a cheeky tourist as much as a hundred feet. Makes for exciting footage on YouTube, though.

GARY FROUBING, RHODE ISLAND

Nope. Although they are commonly believed to sleep standing up, this only came into folklore through the cartoon character 'Jimmy Giraffe', who starred in many early Mortimer (later Mickey) Mouse episodes, alongside others who have vanished such as Clarabelle Cow and Horace Horsecollar. In these cartoons, Jimmy was portrayed as a dozy type who would frequently nod off while guarding trees laden with coconuts that Mortimer so desperately wanted to procure to please his girl, Mabel Mouse.

A typical cartoon would run something like this: after luring Jimmy into slumber (with a potion bought from an eccentric apothecary, in the form of a putative Bugs Bunny, or by performing a hypnotic belly-dance while dressed as a

68

beautiful female giraffe), Mortimer would dispense with him by putting sticks of dynamite up his backside, or sawing his legs off so that he bled to death. Then he would climb up the dead giraffe's neck, retrieve the coconuts and return to Mabel, who would smile at him, while little red hearts rose from her eyes like bubbles. Then the cartoon would cut to a shot of a train going into a tunnel, and finish.

With the mainstream success of more 'friendly' animations these violent comic extravaganzas were hushed up, although Disney continued to commission them for his secret amusement to his dying day. Now only shown at exclusive Hollywood parties, they are the inspiration for *The Simpsons'* Itchy and Scratchy. 'Stag' movies were included in the repertoire, the masterpiece of the sub-genre reportedly being a surprisingly thoughtful film, almost Fellini-esque, explaining the Freudian relationship between Elmer Fudd and Bugs Bunny, and why the hunter discharges his weapon down the rabbit's hole, while Bugs is forever playing hard to get. Rumours that the idea came from the hours Disney used to spend hunting in the woods near his California home are strongly denied by his family.

ANDERSON PETERSON IV, SANTA MONICA

[Ed note: Penelope, you remember that old crinkled envelope I asked you to return to sender? Well, it's been returned to us 'addressee unknown'! And weirder still, the letter inside is different! I'm quite spooked out. Have a read yourself . . .]

Dearest H,

Sorry it's been so long since I wrote. But so much has happened! Honey Tree Cottage is serenely happy, and its three inhabitants are more engrossed than ever in the new life we have found.

Jeremy has been brilliantly productive. He's made a sculpture from some hay called 'Glastonbury bumsocket 179' and is planning to exhibit a ploughshare that was smashed up by some local teens as a piece of found art, cider cans and all. He's going to call it 'Jack Lemmon's Insincere Grin', I think, or 'Lee Van Cleef Chewing a Whip'. I don't pay much attention to his titles, to be honest. He's quite obsessed with rebuilding a little machine he's found in the oldest of our buildings (which might have foundations going back to the Middle Ages), although he won't tell me anything about it.

Petunia, too, is in fine fettle. She spends whole days by the stream with the imaginary friend she made, and while I worry sometimes that she believes in her friend a little too seriously, I know it's just a stage.

But to my main reason for writing – those diaries I've found. The old man who once lived here certainly was a curious fellow! In the entries after he took the little girl under his wing he appears much more agitated and disturbed. It appears that the girl fell sick and died, or she may have fallen into the stream and drowned, I can't tell, and afterwards he felt haunted by her. He spent hours poring over local history records and some demonic parchments he had uncovered in a monastery in Italy, which he is convinced hold the key to releasing him from his curse. I must say, it's more compulsive than a thriller, especially so when I think I catch glimpses of him – Daniel

Dorey is his name – in mirrors, or see his shadow in the next room late at night. (Silly girl!)
I'll write again soon! Once more, your loving,
Clarissa

What is the opposite of 'opposite'?

Minty Chong, Bradford

Wait – this is not so fair. I have still not uncovered whether the answer to your question 'Will your answer to this question be no?' is 'yes' or 'no'. Or whether I am pooing food after eating poo? The opposite of opposite is . . . 'yes'? Or maybe 'the same'. Or 'different', maybe? Wait. Oh *szclaput*.

MILO SVELIC, BRNO, CZECH REP

Why do Americans call sausages-in-a-roll hotdogs? Is this not off-putting?

Roderick Black, Transylvania

Hot dog – I always heard it was something to do with the millionaire press baron William Randolph Hearst. He used to go everywhere with a tiny sausage dog, Mr Pippin, who he dressed in an ermine fur coat, looking for all the world like an enormous frankfurter in a bun. That dog was on the party pages of the *New York Times* every day for a month back in the 1930s, sweltering slowly in a corner of some godforsaken cocktail bar or other; but New Yorkers took him to their hearts and 'hot dogs' in Mr Pippin's honour became quite the most fashionable canapé long before they made their way on to the city's street corners.

LUCY PESSELL, LONDON

Surprised this question was even asked – it's well known that carts serving cheap sausages sticking out of a form of rudimentary dumpling (later replaced by cheap bread rolls) paraded the slums of New Amsterdam in the 1650s. These were invariably pulled by dogs on long leashes, which would pant and sweat with the effort. Much like the sinister siren of a Mr Whippy, the sight of a panting dachshund in harness would signal the appearance in the neighbourhood of the sausage stand (often twenty or thirty feet behind – the dogs were driven on with cruelly long whips) and the first child to spot it would shout 'hot dog!', and be treated to a special relish on top of their snack, a delicious condiment made from the mashed snouts of knackered 'sausage dogs'.

MARK SEARLE, TUMBLEWATER HILL

I'd never heard any of the above, but none of them is true. In fact it came from J. Edgar Hoover's nascent FBI in 1935, where lots of secret messaging systems were used. These included the Blue Bunny (where messages were hidden within packages of children's toys), the Silent Duck (where they were secreted within takeaway Chinese meals) and the Hot Dog (messages that were tied to the collars of specially trained homing spaniels). It is assumed that a disaffected ex-FBI agent caused the name to be leaked to hot frankfurter sellers.

BRYCE SWATCHKOPF, BROOKLYN

How fascinating to see the fantasists above who all seem to believe what they say. In truth, Hot Dog was the name of the third atomic bomb which was to be dropped on Japan, after Little Boy (Hiroshima) and Fat Man (Nagasaki). The raid was threatened to be on Osaka, and was only a few hours shy of commencing when Emperor Hirohito gave the surrender.

BRENT SPOMASTER, BLUE SKY, WYOMING

[Ed note: Penelope, I can't cope with another answer to this question! I thought our column was supposed to help provide true answers to questions, yet all we seem to do is perfectly muddy the waters with a thousand theories! Has it always been this way? By the way, I think those are snail stains, you know, across the back wall. And if my copy of Wildlife Britain *has it right, then the teeth marks on the 'hatstand' stalagmite are those of an otter. Compose a memo, please, to*

the staff of the Young Git, *to be more vigilant when bringing vermin into the office. And next let's attack the far corner of the office, where that horrible plant has been allowed to overgrow. Lord only knows what crimes it hides – I'm sure there are a few more serviceable office chairs under the canopy.]*

How many ways are there to skin a cat?

Mortimer Doley, Drakesburg, Wyoming

142.

DAVID EKELLING, NEUBERG, MISSOURI

167.

AHAB MCSPICE, EASTER ISLANDS, DELIVERED BY QUARTERLY MAIL SHIP

192. How can someone live on some 'islands' – surely only one?

JEROME P. PEROME, MONKSTOWN, EIRE

Typo, sorry.

AHAB MCSPICE, EASTER ISLAND, DELIVERED BY

QUARTERLY MAIL SHIP

My buddy Baldwin has been shaking a stick at Jerome's new record these six months. He's determined, and he's got a whole community of cat lovers living in fear. His trailer's uninhabited and he's living wild and outlawed on meal scraps and mice, snatching the pussies with torn curtain strips doused in catnip and stretching their skins across the mouth of the cave he's dug in the local refuse pit. I've seen him in there – somebody stop him!

HARRY BUTE OSWESTER, TRUTH OR CONSEQUENCES, NEW MEXICO

193.

BALDWIN MAKEPEACE THURSGOOD, TRUTH OR CONSEQUENCES,

NEW MEXICO

We've become very concerned that this question has ignited a lot of cat hate in a wide variety of areas. The skinning of domestic cats was largely discontinued in the late eighteenth century but carried on in secret with cat fur being faked for rarer animals such as ermine, mink, sable and (occasionally) fox. But it's the *nature* of the question that troubles us. The traditional method of cat skinning (making a circular incision around the cat's nose, then peeling the rest back in a sharp movement) was recently countered with a new procedure from Turkmenistan. This was cutting in a circle around the cat's midriff and pulling sharply in either direction. And yet, in *Cat Quarterly*, I read of a further barbaric innovation in the field of taxidermy that hails from Malaysia: first making an incision around the cat's anus, the whole skin is pulled 'upwards' from there, the furrier holding the cat down by hooking his finger around the inside of the arsehole. Sometimes they even kill the cat first. I provide these details to show what is being done all around us all the time. Please help us stop the cat madness.

PROF. JEFFREY SCOLE, PRESIDENT, LEAGUE FOR THE
PROTECTION OF CATS

194.

BALDWIN MAKEPEACE THURSGOOD, TRUTH OR CONSEQUENCES,
NEW MEXICO

Dear Sir, as someone who has always loved the natural world, but knows next to nothing about it, I recently purchased a copy of your book entitled *Do Ants Have Arseholes? and 101 other bloody ridiculous questions*. I expected lots of interesting facts about cute animals, so you can imagine my horror at discovering it was a disgusting agglomeration of depravity and stupidity written by a bunch of deranged morons. Not at all like all the other books I own with 'arseholes' in the title, which are

interesting and helpful to a fault. Is a public apology
forthcoming, and a withdrawal of the book?

LANCE FRIBBER, BASINGSTOKE

Dear Mr Fribber (are you related to the Salisbury Fribbers
by any chance? I might have gone to Eton with your cousin
Sandy! 'Gobstopper' we used to call him – oh to be a
sexually adventurous fourteen-year-old again!),
Alas, the exigencies of the book publishing process make
withdrawal of the first volume in this collection impossible.
And I can't publicly apologise, you understand, due to the
fact that those 'morons' (as you call them, although
between us you understate the case) are our faithful
readership. So, apologetic as I am, and alarmed as I
continue to be by the responses to our letters page, this
letter will have to do.
With regret,
The Editor, *Old Git* magazine

*[Ed note: Penelope, type and send the above, please. Of
course Fribber sums up my feelings exactly but I can't
advertise it in print: we must soldier on with these weirdos.
By the way, I have noticed that you've made a special effort
with your clothes of late, and it is regrettable that the Lord
Mayor's visit and photo-shoot fell on a dress-down Friday.
The hour we had to spend locking away all the booze and
rude pictures that belonged to my predecessor was bad
enough, but if I'd known that ordering you to change your
'I'm not as Think as You Drunk I am!' T-shirt for your photo
with him would make you slip into one that read 'I'm with*

this c*nt→, I never would have done it. I do wish you would
be more sensitive to politics (office and otherwise)
sometimes. Oh, plus I phoned the Co-op to ask why we've
had no milk this week and apparently Barry (was that his
name?) has been MURDERED, horrifyingly, and the police
have no idea why, or who did it. I've been drinking black tea
all day out of respect . . .]

I s there any connection between the telephone-related expressions 'Give someone a ring' and 'Being engaged'?

Lawrence Dogwat, Manchester

Ahah! But I have always wondered what connection there might be between the place being called Liver*pool* and a person from there being a Liver*puddl*ian! Is there some fiddly historical-biographical explanation which somehow involves poo/violence to animals/sexual deviancy with which someone might elucidate us?

SAMUEL FERN, EDENBRIDGE

To me, ringing home to hear the engaged tone has always meant that my cheating shitbag, sexually incompetent

78

husband Leonard is on the blower to one of his braindead pipsqueak teenage tarts. 'Engaged' means 'engaged in cowardly betrayal'; 'giving a ring' means 'giving a plastic piece of tat from Accessorize to try and get a shag from the barmaid at Wetherspoons'. But perhaps that's just my reaction.

DEBORAH MEWS, SLOUGH

Oh Deborah, I know just where you're coming from. Only two nights ago I heard about tensions on the border of the Gaza Strip. I thought to myself, this is *exactly* the sort of thing that sod Leonard always lets happen, it's typical, it wouldn't surprise me if he allowed it to escalate into full-scale war. The next morning, what do you know – three thousand Israeli troops invade! Deborah, you have my sympathy and that of every other long-suffering wife in the country. I don't know how you put up with him for so long.

LESLEY BANGULOE, KETTERING

[Ed note: Penelope, once more I'm not entirely comfortable with our readers laying the blame for all and sundry at this Mr Mews's door. It smacks of bullying. Please publish no more letters from Mrs Mews. And BY THE WAY, did you speak to the impertinent and despicable Marc yesterday? He marched into my office as cocky as you please wearing some extraordinary garment on his lower half which was either absurdly long shorts or ridiculously short trousers, but looked ugly either way, and explained to me that the Young Git *is not a sister publication but a replacement for us! I was horrified as he explained that we were being 'wound down' and that*

he'd appreciate it if the 'petty acts of sabotage' came to a halt. Had no idea what he was talking about but apparently they've had several resignations due to hate messages, their office furniture being sawed up during the night and false adverts having been placed in trade journals appealing for 'typical cocksucking London media shits'. As my granddaughter would say: WHATEVER. That's his problem. Oh, one more thing, could you hear that dreadful banging around in the office below us yesterday? Go down and ask them to keep a lid on it, would you? I'd be very grateful.]

Did the 1969 moon landing really happen?

Roger Kensall, Argyll

Rupy Belmullet's answer, in a previous issue of the *Old Git*, takes it for granted that Apollo 11 reached the moon. In fact, many people have highlighted the photographic anomalies of the '69 landing: the images of a US flag proudly flapping in the breeze (impossible in a vacuum); the fact that a footprint would not be left in near-weightless moon dust; and the shot of Neil Armstrong sipping a Martini while sitting, legs dangling, on a beachball-sized Earth, as Buzz Aldrin 'moons' the citizens of the watching world. I don't know about the technical stuff, but the latter can be dismissed right away; it was almost certainly taken in Christmas 1969 at the Houston office party – a legendary annual blast where hardened astronauts could unwind from the endless drills of the other 360-odd days of the year. The full contact sheet of photographs from the '69 bash is quite something. In one, a laughing Michael Collins holds a wheel of Edam next to the moon, mugging a puzzled expression, while Apollo controller Ed Finch holds two identical cheeses as 'breasts' over his T-shirt; in another, Armstrong surprises Aldrin with a custard pie to the face and (according to a recently discovered audio recording) delivers a speech to the waiting world: 'This is one small step for man, this is custard's last stand . . . You people make me, you make me . . . the Martinis . . . I love you people, I just feel sick. I didn't want to go to no moon, but gimme a night with Raquel Welch and I'll bench press old Selene for you, Control, you hear me? I'm king of this goddamn world.' It should be noted that none of the astronauts, in any of these shots, is wearing anything other than a T-shirt bearing the legend 'My pal Neil went to the moon and all he brought back was this lousy T-shirt'.

RANDY MCFADDEN, FLORIDA

When they make bubble-wrap in the factory, what do they pack it in?

Gav Dundee, Holy Island

What a lovely question, 'Gav' (is that pronounced 'gave'? Most unusual.) It's weird to think it now, but when it was invented in the 1970s by art handlers at the Louvre in Paris, bubble-wrap was one of the most expensive materials per gram on the planet, lying fourth behind diamond, weapons-grade plutonium and Blue Nun white wine. At the time it was seen as a miracle of engineering that could be used to transport, say, a Van Gogh masterpiece, but was vastly beyond the means of most normal people. Counter-intuitive as it may seem, the best way to transport bubble-wrap to and from art galleries, then, was to encase it in cut-glass crystal fruit bowls. As with a modern cycling helmet, which is designed to break on impact (thus saving the spongy, soft head of the cyclist), the bowls would shatter, leaving the bubble-wrap largely unpopped.

CLAUDIA RAINIER, ASQUITH GALLERY, LEWES

Further to Claudia's answer: bubble-wrap, of course, was the subject of the very first winner of the Turner Prize, back in 1987. Elisa Carston's *Bubble wrap wrapped* – 'Space wrapped within space, wrapped within space; a metaphor for the intangible protection of a long-dead God', as one critic had it – has long been heralded as a conceptual masterpiece, the natural successor to Piero Manzoni's tin of 'artist's shit' and a key influence on Martin Creed's *Work No. 79, some Blu-tack kneaded, rolled into a ball and depressed against a wall* (1993) – widely acclaimed as one of the greatest feats of design since the construction of St Peter's Cathedral in Rome, or Chartres in France.

GEORGINA MORLEY, LONDON

Would it help global warming to leave my fridge door open?

Mr Plum, Plumstead

[Ed note: I'll say it again, Penelope, I like the cut of this man Plum's jib. Please order up a hundred ice lollies from Antonio the local ice cream man, and have the cleaning staff walk around with them. I'd like to see those young gits complain about our carbon footprint then.]

I was confused by the letter from Mr Plum. I think it is supposed to be 'global warning', not 'global warming'. Does anyone know what we are being warned about? Words are confusing. I picked up the last *Old Git* book and it was just words words words. Please don't publish my letter, I'm even fed up of seeing these words here that I'm writing. And those ones. Stop it.

UNMARKED ENVELOPE

How preposterous. The ludicrous lefty rags have got it into their heads that the world is somehow 'endangered' by our advanced industrial development. No doubt they'd all like us to live in reed-thatched huts and poo into streams. No one seems to have noticed that all this fuss originated with a supposedly harmless Hollywood entertainment called *The Day After Tomorrow* starring Al Gore (who looks so much more relaxed since his split from Meg Ryan). In it an absurd apocalypse is visited upon the metropolises of the earth because a few busy individuals occasionally use processed cheese, or disposable nappies. A little common sense is called for, I think! And as for the smoking ban, don't get me st

EDGE OF LETTER SINGED OFF; FORWARDED AS THE ONLY SURVIVING DOCUMENT FROM THE FIRE THAT DEVOURED FIFTEEN RETIREMENT DWELLINGS IN WESTON-SUPER-MARE LAST WEEK, KILLING SIXTY-FIVE.

Don't listen to a word of the above letter! The planet is in trouble, my friends – close that fridge, switch that TV off at the mains! In my recent travels I have seen such terrifying sights as polar bears paddling in New York bay, Inuits wearing flip-flops and Bermuda shorts, and districts in Mexico employing gondolas instead of taxis! This threat is real and getting worse by the day. Don't wait for the waters to lap at your door.

N. COGNITO, MEXICO

[Me again, Penny! Don't type up any of the postscripts on my dashing nom de guerre's missives, I need hardly tell you. The true identity of N. Cognito must remain – you know, what's the word?

Anyway, the above answer really is true, you know. The North Pole is now only a three-mile march from the edge of

the thinning ice shelf, I was terrified to discover. After
planting a Union Jack – from which hung a jewelled pendant
showing the young Queen Victoria, as you would expect – I
made my way south on a Japanese whaling ship.
CHARMING *people, but found the huge amount of rice had*
its ramifications. My colon felt like a child's party balloon
for three weeks – you know, the sort that's thirty feet long
and gets twisted into the shape of a poodle. Anyway, turned
out the Japanese sailors used copies of our venerable
magazine to wipe down the winding mechanism of their
harpoon. Something about the uniquely porous paper we
use – you must congratulate Chris Gibson in Production
(does he still run the department from his hip bath, opium
pipe in hand?) for winning us subscriptions to the entire
whaling fleets of Norway and Japan. Reading the actual
thing, I have to say – the new editor! Is he up to the job?
Sounds like a prissy little madam to me. This Young Git
business – why does he not fight with tooth and claw? If you
value anything good and true, Penny, you know what you
must do – become an undercover agent. Make friends with
them, and obliterate their operation from within, although if
I know you well enough you will have done so from the start!
Oh, how I long to be back in the chair, my unsocked feet
ruffling the eyebrows of that tiger I brained with a bedpan in
Bengal!

To keep you up to date with my travels, travelling through
the Caribbean, the whaler ran into some stick with
bothersome Greenpeace types.(Rather a shame – I had been
doing so well on the video console game Captain Miyazaki
had me play, where you had to hit the moving shapes with
darting arrows. It reminded me of my grandson Freddy's Xbox,
which I bought him so I could play on it. Thoughtless present

*for a blind child, perhaps.) I swam ashore and climbed a
mountain to find a most fascinating tribe of Central
American natives, as yet undestroyed – and undiscovered, so
far as I can tell, although one of them had a rather snazzy
toaster – by Western civilisation. Something in my aspect
struck them as regal, a charge I did not demur, and I write this
from a gold throne atop a stone temple. I am fed six times a
day and worshipped with hardly less regularity. All terribly
droll – they even act out little dramas, pretending to sacrifice
young men to me in remarkably convincing fashion. One of
the more worshipful servants, a chap called Armal, has
promised to get me out of here when I've grown bored with the
whole thing, but for now it's like a lovely holiday. And then
there are the virgins, which I . . . well, I . . . well . . .]*

Did curiosity really kill the cat?

Chantal Christmas, Penguinstown, Nova Scotia

Curiosity has, it goes without saying, killed a good many
cats over the years. While working as a floor manager on
Animal Hospital with Rolf Harris, I witnessed some very
sorry scenes – the dreadful stink and mess that greeted us
every morning on-set was enough to make me gag – but we
always managed to get Rolf cleaned up in time for the

cameras to roll. The range of cat accidents was quite astonishing, though. One poor, starved kitty whose owner lived in Portsmouth had chased a delicious mouse into one of those big, wine-making glass bottles, which rolled down the hill from the pavement recycling bin and into the English channel. Fortunately, before it could sink, a local child fished it out, thinking it was a message in a bottle. The child got quite a shock; but the doctors can do wonders with disfigured noses nowadays. Another cat from the first series stumbled into the Hogmanay celebrations in Edinburgh and spent an evening being squeezed under a Scotsman's arm before he realised the mistake. I don't know which bit of the cat he tried to blow into, but Rolf was particularly upset by that one . . . Happy days!

SAMANTHA JAMES, SURREY QUAYS

Dear Sir, I have been a dedicated subscriber to the *Old Git* for many years. I enjoy the detached style of reportage and comment, find the cartoons page delightful (especially Tarby the Spastic Elephant! Will he *ever* stop losing his keys? The silly spastic!) and became addicted to Gen Smythington-Smythe's hilarious globetrotting racism – my children love him too. But that was until I was driven to write in a few times recently over responses in this column which could technically qualify as 'cat hate'. Distressed by these, I gave up my subscription until a friend showed me the above entry, and I have to re-subscribe in a new capacity: cat-watcher. I acknowledge this proliferation of cat-violence literature may not be an editorial policy, and at a stretch could be outrageous coincidence, but in truth so many of

87

your correspondents write in with stories which revolve around cat abuse that I fear your publication has struck upon the very demographic we at the League for the Protection of Cats have been trying to eradicate all these years: cat-haters.

Take Samantha's entry above: was there any need to go into such detail? No! But worse – much worse, and infinitely damning – casting aside the magazine as I read it, it landed next to Mrs Cadwallader, a nervous Siamese. She instinctively hissed at it – the cat hate rose from it like a noxious gas – and she fled through the cat flap into the road where a speeding lorry braked too late, jack-knifing and toppling its cargo of chemical waste on to the cat sanctuary we had lobbied for twenty years to have built next door to the office. All the cats perished except one – a wily survivor named Uncle who now has *two* limps and an even more wicked glint in his one good eye. He sits on my lap and I stroke my tears from his fur as I write this. Stop it! Please, please stop the cat hate!

PROF. JEFFREY SCOLE, PRESIDENT, LEAGUE FOR THE
PROTECTION OF CATS

[Ed note: Great panreligious deity, Penelope! The things we stir up. Send flowers, would you, to Professor Scole, and a note of abjectest apology, if abjectest is a word. Funny thing is, I'd been using that funny rag left by the old editor as a shoe cloth until I spotted that it had not only a tail, but a collar with a little bell! Poor Mopsy. Plus (why are you never at your desk? I seem to do nothing except leave notes for you) quelle horreur about the folks downstairs. I never knew them, but still – do the police know whether it happened while we were in the office? How awful . . . I heard the two officers talking at the door saying, 'Three of them . . . in the bath . . . with a hacksaw'. I've always wanted to climb over POLICE

TAPE: DO NOT CROSS, *but now that I have to each morning, the blood runs cold. In other news: three new offensives from that total cat Marc at the* Young Git: *he proposes exchanging Tarby the Spastic Elephant with a cartoon about a 'pilled-up polar bear' or some such crap; he wants Gen. Smythington-Smythe's column to be replaced by the assembled reflections of something called a brand recognition analyst (that does sound interesting, though – they've managed to make a machine that can talk and write?); and he doesn't think we need an opera correspondent at all! Imagine if Olivietta found out. The fat lady really would sing then. Mealy-mouthed, small minded little philistine! I'll fight this to the top!]*

Corrections & Clarfications

In last month's 'Ed Note', which shouldn't have been published anyway, although that's by the by, the editor did not intend to refer to the editor of the *Young Git* as a 'total cat'. However, he desires that the word he did intend to use does not make its way into print on any accunt.

From the same issue: in the column of Gen Smythington-Smythe's reminiscences about smoking opium under the shadow of the sphinx, many readers have complained about the sentence which read, 'The Nubian slave girl who served us skewers of cat meat once the heavenly reverie had passed, performed an expressive and extravagantly erotic dance, and I procured her favours for fifty Egyptian pounds'. The word 'Nubian' should indeed have read 'nubile'.

Has the sort of chocolate money you get at Christmas ever been legal tender?

Billy Braithwaite, aged ten, Godalming

Indeed it has, Billy. During the Great Depression of '29 'real' money was very hard to come by, but an overproduction of chocolate money and sweets in 1928 led to a glut of the stuff that sustained many families trapped in the Dust Bowl with no work or prospects.

Not surprisingly, gangsters from Boston, Chicago and New York soon spotted the wealth of the new market and a host of new anti-heroes was created: the gluttonous bank-robber Sam 'Baby Cakes' Snicker (to whom we owe the now-famous chocolate brand name); Bugsy Truffle, with his big fat face and chocolate-fountain speakeasies in the Queens district of New York; and Fats Slim, best known for his 'yo-yo diet' monthly raids on the chocolate bank in Main Street, Ohio, and subsequent purges at a remote health farm. All three men left a trail of violence and foil wrappers across the US, waddling their way to criminal immortality. Of course, the sugar crash of 1930 brought an end to all that – and all three men went to gaol owing hundreds-and-thousands in tax.

LASHAUNTEA ISHMAEL ALLAJOWAN,
STOKE-ON-TRENT

I don't know if it's legal or not, but I've been paying my son Wayne's pocket money in chocolate coins for several months now, to teach him the real worth of money. The experiment got off to a bad start when he ate £47.50 in chocolate pennies he'd found in the kitchen drawer, but since then he's been saving hard, and the doctor says his normal colour will return soon.

DAVID SPOKES, COVENTRY

Corrections & Clarfications

Last month we printed an article about the ex-Saudi footballer turned Cairo chef Hgalib mu-Bhafan m'sahash'Bupha. He phoned to point out that our reporter had it wrong and that he had in fact been a helicopter pilot in Cairo and not a chef after all. We would like to apologise to Mr mu-Bhafan m'sahash'Buhpa for this, and for the fact that we've almost certainly spelt his name wrong in some way. It's probably not good form to say this, but we humbly suggest that he doesn't phone again with the correct spelling, as it was a terribly crackly line from Egypt and it would be likely to result in further apologies of this sort.

Who was the first person to fall off a bike?

Mandy P P P P P P P P bastard keyboard Spillane

I don't know the name of the first person to fall off a bike, but I can tell you they were blind. The idea of attaching two wheels in a frame and placing a saddle above them first came to an English country vicar, Dr Archibald Seaburst, in the late 1650s as a way to transport his blind, obese sister. The contraptions quickly caught on and blind people all around the countryside could be seen being led to church, or to town, on them. But when it came to the attention of Oliver Cromwell's parliament that there was a huge number of deaths due to their use, an investigation explained the cause for their popularity. In an England deprived of theatre, gambling and every kind of vice under Cromwell's puritanical leadership, groups of young men were finding blind people to send down hills on the contraptions as a form of entertainment. A typical situation would be a village hill with a pond at the bottom, abutted by a wall. The boys would send the poor sightless people careening down and take bets on whether they would reach the pond, fall off or smash into the wall. Often two or more were raced against each other.

Without such cruel sport, the blind poet John Milton might never have written so fiercely and immediately of Satan's fall from grace. But puritanism won out, and bicycles were immediately banned. It was fifty years before it occurred to anyone to resurrect them for non-blind people.

BOB SMART, STUTTERFIELD

A re there any rules or guidelines as to what racehorses can be called?

Paolo Egremont, Leicester

A racehorse is not allowed to be named after a swearword, a trademarked company or a member of the Danish Royal Family (owing to a curious subclause in a trade treaty from 1821). Apart from that, anything goes. It's been the pet hate of the racing industry these last few years that silly names have come into fashion. This began after the highly respected trainer James Gallaway had a breakdown in 2001 and began renaming his horses after the creatures he imagined were trying to get down his chimney to, as he put it in an unprompted letter to *The Times*, 'appease the evil spirits and prevent them chewing on my hairy bottomcheeks'. He raced them under their new names ('Slumgullion' and 'Slurping Ticklepest' were two) to the abject horror of the horses' owners.

This quickly became a fad, especially after the notorious eccentric and alcoholic Sir Henry Rawlins-Sunshine bought out the stables and the entire stock of the bankrupt Kent-based Percy Blister. Rawlins-Sunshine took great delight in giving his horses stupid or humiliating names such as 'Chief Mangosuthu Buthelezi', 'Jewish Conspiracy' and 'I Hate Horses'. The fashion spread until by the middle of the flat racing season of 2004 John

McCririck's commentaries began to sound like a kind of Dadaist poetry, and to be written down and posted on the internet by Goldsmiths College students as instances of found art.

JOSEPH CANDISCAPE, ST ALBANS

As a corollary to the above question, are there rules about what photographs are put up outside cheap eateries (mostly fast food joints and low-grade pubs) as to how closely they should resemble the food on offer?

Harrison Spender, Ashby-de-la-Zouch

This is a fad that began in Japan, where to this day one of the delightful quirks of travelling there is seeing extremely intricate models of food outside the copious street-side restaurants. As with our photos of sizzling burgers and over-stuffed kebabs, they're often more inviting than the food itself. The main difference is that they're crafted out of plastic. The European vogue for almost sleazily alluring photos of food came out of Amsterdam, after porn kingpin Laurens Van Horten experienced a Damascene conversion when a massive track full of pornography he was driving careered off a bridge and he survived.

He converted to Catholicism as he surveyed the wreckage on the roadside, and walked away, leaving seventy thousand copies of *80+ Gagging Old Slags* magazine, much to the disgust of the residents of Eindhoven (and the deep disappointment of local adolescent boys, whose dreams, they felt, had so nearly come true).

Thereafter he took his gaudy, over-lit aesthetic into food photography, where he has proved equally successful. His grimy studios in the centre of Amsterdam's whore zone became a hive of activity and a destination for foodies worldwide. Aside from his generic low-grade pizza and fried chicken set-ups (a factory conveyor-belt system that he nevertheless fastidiously oversaw, allegedly getting into a romantic relationship with the star hamburger who he signed to a massive thousand-picture contract for a then-exorbitant fee), he produced high-class glossy illustrations for all the great celebrity chefs. Gossip abounded in the food world about his techniques to capture the right look, from using gloss paint instead of cream, to constructing huge thirty-foot bowls of soup to give 'epic depth of vision' to Jamie's meaty broth. Either way, there is no doubt he gave birth to what we now know as 'food porn'.

ALVIN HOLE, EXMOUTH

What exactly is Davy Jones's locker?

Anna Carmichael, London

'Davy Jones' of Davy Jones's locker fame is often supposed
to be the well-known contortionist and ascetic Dai
Llewellyn Jones, who made a name for himself in the
theatres, illicit bear-pits and secretive cock-fighting dens of
the Scottish Lowlands in the late eighteenth century. He

reputedly had a Houdini-like facility to dislocate his limbs painlessly and clamber into or out of small spaces.

A terrifyingly thin man with a prickly ginger beard and a birthmark in the shape of the boot of Italy over his oesophagus, he was naturally shy, and having grown up in a carpenter's shop he felt most comfortable sleeping folded (rather than curled) up in a chest drawer. His highly popular act involved his assistant Fortescue (a syphilitic rogue grotesquely made up as a grinning minstrel) opening and shutting drawers in a large chest as Jones appeared or disappeared with apparent impossibility – his grinning mug emerging from the bottom drawer, his left foot from the top one. The act made his name famous although it was never deemed apt for any larger arena than the local flea-pits, and his and Fortescue's reward (which they shared equally) never escalated above the brief shower of pennies that came down from the crowd as they waited for the baited bear to come on.

By his early forties, his joints tired with the effort and starting to suffer the effects of syphilis he may have caught from the now dead Fortescue (neither ever married), the paper trail of Jones's appearances dries up in the Dundee area. He had taken to performing cheap and very uncomfortable spectaculars for which he received poor financial returns – encasing himself in ice for three days, hanging by his nipples from the Firth of Forth Bridge – until in desperation he announced he would be publicly chained into a locker and thrown into the bay. On an icy winter's day, a sparse crowd gathered to watch this happen, and when the box hit the water let out a weak cheer. When the bubbles had cleared and half an hour had passed, the sharp North Sea wind began to bite and their hopes of a spectacle fading, the group drifted away.

James Boswell passed through the city a week later and heard the story from a desultory lonely drinker in the corner of a tavern. Enquiring in horror why no one had tried to save the doomed contortionist, he writes that the drinker stared at him, blinked, punched him in the face, and returned to his pint of whisky.

GWEN MCDONALD, KIRKCUDBRIGHT

How far are method actors supposed to go to research a part? If they are playing the part of a murderer, do they have to kill someone?

Kathy Tarkle, Lewisham

You're opening a CAN OF WORMS with this question, Kathy, a can of worms. Because it's widely known in film circles that a certain actor who recently won Best Actor Oscar – let's call him, erm, Daniel *Night*-Lewis – did just that.

The long hiatus after his box-office and critical disappointment with *The Boxer*, was not, as his publicity team insisted, because he was retired. Quite the opposite. It was the busiest period of his career, working on several projects that did not get off the ground.

Firstly there was a fiasco with legendary *Badlands*

filmmaker Terrence Malick's adaptation of William Golding's novel *The Inheritors*, which describes ape-like humans trying to survive at the dawn of time. The second he heard it, Night-Lewis threw the phone down, stripped off his clothes and ran off to live wild in the hills above Mulholland Drive. Although he survived remarkably well, he eventually ate a poisonous and hallucinogenic mushroom and hill walkers stumbled upon him standing on his hands and pretending to be the five of clubs.

Next, Michael Mann appeared at Night-Lewis's hospital bedside to offer him the part of the real-life Gallic master art thief Raymond Le Mesutier. The following morning the nurse came in to find Night-Lewis's bed empty, and the window open. There was no sign as to how he had descended the sheer thirty-storey façade except for a missing packet of paper clips and a hospital gown with one sleeve torn off.

The police quickly realised the magnitude of what had been unleashed on an unsuspecting art world and one of the biggest manhunts in history was started. He was finally apprehended by Interpol from a helicopter as he was sliding down an improvised zip wire onto the roof of the Louvre. In his back pocket was a copy of the blueprints, with a dotted line leading to the *Mona Lisa*.

But worse was to come. Even though the above incidents were widely known in Hollywood (although they'd been effectively silenced in the media), Quentin Tarantino got it into his head that Night-Lewis would be perfect for the central role in a biopic of blond-haired psychotic vigilante Kramer Blatt, a Vietnam vet who had raised hell against the Colombian drug barons who had killed his daughter. Tarantino had said as much to Empire magazine in 1997: 'It would be SO COOL to work with that guy! I'd be like jizzing my pants with excitement every motherfucking minute, coz it'd be like SO COOL, you know?' Tarantino, who was educated at Harvard and Oxford, had written a screenplay that paid homage to the vigilante movies of the 1970s like *Dirty Harry* and *Death Wish*, and sent Night-Lewis a copy.

The ensuing slaughter of over four hundred drug lords, their minions, servants and all their friends and family (as, Tarantino ruefully admitted, was stipulated in his script) was met with hesitant admiration by the Colombian Minister of the Interior. 'Certainly,' he admitted, 'the traffic in cocaine has been damaged by these actions. But Colombian TV won't be showing *My Left Foot* any time soon.'

HARVEY WINEGARDEN, SACRAMENTO

Corrections & Clarfications

Unfortunately, last month's apology to the well-known ex-Saudi helicopter pilot, ex-Cairo animal husbandrist turned New York drag act Hgalib al-Bhafan m'sahasg 'Baphu provoked a rush of further complaints. From Mr al-Bhafan m'sahash'Bupha himself, for spelling his name wrong *again* (which we have done our best to correct here, although we're not holding out too much hope) and to the owner of the name we used – one Mr mu-Bafhan m'sahash'Bupha, who is in fact a Senegalese-born mural painter turned Muslim cleric. We apologise for any inconvenience caused to either gentleman, and especially to Mr mu-Bhafan m'sahash 'Bupha, for not taking him seriously the first four times he phoned. We hope the case of Veuve Clicquot we biked over to his mosque redresses the insult.

Why is it that, whenever a big West End show opens, some journalist always comes up with a review that contains exactly the sort of line (usually a pun) which the show's producers would want to advertise with? Am I right to detect money changing hands?

Isaac Twemlow, Edinburgh

That is a terrible and cynical thing to posit! As a successful producer of musicals such as *Fungus the Bogeyman* and *Eureka!* (the comedy extravaganza based on the life of Archimedes), I'd like to point out that Isaac probably doesn't realise that the writing, rehearsals, costumes and sets of a major West End musical can cost as much as a Hollywood movie. So, when the first night comes round, it's a minuscule expense to send chauffeured limousines for the reviewers and serve them champagne in the foyer. It's only natural that we invite them backstage to meet the most talented and beautiful performers. And it is unavoidable that over time friendships form, and that I am able to provide personal friendly gifts to help them, whether it is a fortnight in my mansion in the Bahamas, or a paid companion to visit them at their homes and help fill up the aching chasm of guilt and loneliness which fills their souls. After that, if they choose to give a good review, it is entirely down to them.

TINY VENABLES, FRITH STREET, LONDON

Quite the opposite effect on reviewers was something that my dear friend, the actor Charles Paris was afflicted with. Although a staunch performer in rep and a solid actor (not to mention a thoroughly decent chap and a stalwart supporter of Bell's Whisky), there was something about the man that excited the ire of almost every critic to witness him in action.

When playing Hedda Gabler's husband at the Old Vic in Bristol in 1983, one reviewer said, 'The culminating tragedy of Ibsen's masterpiece was diffused for this viewer by thoroughgoing sympathy with her plight at being married to such a bore, and by the desire that she shoot him instead'. His Falstaff in *Henry IV Part I* at the Guildford Yves Arnaud Theatre was described thus: 'Never have I been less convinced of the joviality of a rogue. Never have I been less persuaded by a mischievous charmer's ability to lead others into trouble. Never have I been more convinced of a character being utterly, thoroughly pissed.'

The worst came, though, when Paris had a very brief stint on Channel Five in the title role of a rival to ITV's series of *Poirot*, which came about due to a dispute over the rights to several of the short stories. Of the pilot episode (which was never followed up) the TV critic Nancy Banks-Smith said, 'I watched it all in a serene and dream-like state. When it had finished I unplugged my TV, carried it upstairs, filled my bath, and dropped it in.'

WARNOCK BELVEDERE, TANGIERS

The producers of West End shows should count themselves lucky that (one presumes) the reviewers watch the shows at all! For twenty-five years the *Old Git* was cursed with a book reviewer who steadfastly refused to read the books that landed on his desk and analysed them only by the cover. A lazy, arrogant and unhappy Ernald Broadhurst was secured the job by the outgoing editor, Herbert Longleat Christhorn Murledew, who signed him up on a lifetime contract from his deathbed in 1965.

His weakness for relying on reviews he had read elsewhere (and not very thoroughly) quickly became apparent. He incorrectly supposed the 'sex-crazed' nature of *Portnoy's Complaint* was not of a heterosexual persuasion, and dismissed it as a 'vile outpouring of the tumescent society of sodomites gathered in Manhattan's own Gomorrah'.

Despite hundreds of letters of complaint the editorial chiefs were powerless to remove the eccentric. As the years wore on his alcoholism grew worse and his reviews fared no better. He greeted the publication of *One Hundred Years of Solitude* with: 'Surely the most boring book ever written. It is amazing that this tale of a centenarian who has lived ten decades without meeting a single soul was ever published, let alone translated. It has no redeeming feature.'

In his last days he became a favourite of readers who bought the *Old Git* to see what he would get wrong next. Alas, his alcoholism gaining ground, eventually he was submitting barely comprehensible copy and giving no protest when it got rejected. He achieved his swansong, though, to the delight of his fans, when he hilariously delivered a long, loving paean of praise to *Oranges Are Not the Only Fruit*. It's said he was confined to hospital soon afterwards and actually read the book. Realising what he had done, he never wrote again, although he continued to be paid by the magazine. He died five years later.

TIMOFEY NINP, LITERARY CRITIC OF THE *OLD GIT*, LONDON

Corrections & Clarfications
It gives us great pain to confess that our apologies to
the ex-Congolese footballer, ex-Saudi helicopter chef,
ex-New York drag queen turned London media pundit
Hgalib mu-Bhafan m'sahash'Bapuh have proved
insufficient, and have caused him such great personal
distress. Our legal department – or Kerry, as she's
known – advises us that we can no longer make
assurances that we will spell people's names correctly.
We would also like to point out that those of us who
write this corrections column are not, as he claimed in
his last letter, 'paid by the fucking word'. However it
gives us great relief to announce that, having
recovered from his recent nervous breakdown, he has
changed his name to Terry Smith. Good decision, Mr
al-Bhafna m'saash'Bupha!

Is it possible to suck yourself off without
putting your back out? Have you got the
number of any chiropractors?

Henry Gaylord, Guildford

No – but these days, there's no need to try! In today's stressful twenty-four-hour culture of all work and no play, who has time to meet a suitable mate? And if not, why forgo the delights of oral sex? A daring and exciting new programme has been set up by Udolf Von Strattenberg, a pioneering surgeon and practitioner of the sexual arts, who travels the Netherlands in his mobile operating room performing his special 'blow surgery' for a high price. No more tearful dreams of having been born some kind of onanist Houdini (and heaven knows what he got up to!) – Udolf simply removes four vertebrae from your spine to allow access to pleasure! Book an appointment today. And no, I don't have the number of any chiropractors, Henry, sorry. Try leaning backwards over a settee and coughing violently, it worked for my poor dead dad.

ELSIE LEPPING, STAFF NURSE, VIA EMAIL

[Ed note: Penelope, I detect the sordid mentality of my predecessor in the above question and/or answer. I trust you do not recognise the handwriting and that you would tell me if you did, hateful as his memory must be? Also, please get Consuela to clear out the contents of the filing cabinet's third drawer. I like to think that he collected so many hundreds of cards from telephone boxes in the interests of cleaning up the area, but I fear the worst. Plus, looking in the fourth drawer I found it contained a tiny, perfectly proportioned bouncy castle, almost as if it were for a mouse! So he had a fondness for every kind of local wildlife, eh?]

W ho designs the interiors of sitcom flats, and chooses all the vases and furniture that 'belong' to Frasier, Jerry Seinfeld, etc.?

Philip Gribaldi, Phoenix

On most of these shows this job is done, quite simply, by a set designer. The cast do sometimes have a say, however, and trivia fans might like to know that Martin Crane's famous easy-chair on *Frasier* actually belongs to the tiny actor who has played Martin's dog 'Eddie' with such distinction over the years. More interesting, though, are the rumours that have circulated in TV land for a decade now – almost a ghost story, if you will – about the mysterious owner of Monica Geller's flat in *Friends*.

So the story goes, back in the 1950s a hopeful wannabe actress named Margaret du Bois had tried, and failed, to be signed up by any of the big light-entertainment shows of the day. *I Love Lucy, The Ricky Fontalia Show, An Evening with Spanky Markovitz* – Du Bois auditioned for them all and despite her immaculate dress and manners, she lost out every time to younger, prettier actresses with more experience and feet that pointed the right way. Cursing the gods and her poor, backward-facing feet, Margaret is said to have retreated to a warehouse storeroom on the lot of Paramount Studios, venturing out only to pilfer meagre rations from the studio canteen, nursing her bitterness over the years and pouring her creative energy instead into making a home of the cold, dark storeroom.

Now as it goes, Margaret had exquisite taste and a fine eye for interior decoration. She had lost her other eye many years earlier, on Spanky Markovitz's casting couch, but for once her bad luck did not deter her in her mission. As the fifties became the sixties, she slowly begged, borrowed and stole pieces from the sets of Paramount films; a porcelain greyhound from the party scene of *Breakfast at Tiffany's* here, a vase from *The Fall of the Roman Empire* there. Ranging wider through the backlots of Hollywood, she took magnificent Albert Whitlock scenery paintings of the New York skyline at night, and put them just outside the windows of the warehouse to create the illusion of a view. For ten hours a day, every day through the sixties, seventies, eighties, Margaret worked at creating the perfect homely flat, stopping only to peep out of the spyhole in her lavender front door with her one good eye, ever more mindful of the outside world.

In time, the flat was finished. Margaret's feet ached like never before and she became a true recluse, her wild hair white, driven half mad by loneliness and seclusion, still wearing the old audition dress from the 1950s. Now framed with gold, the spyhole became her only window on the world as she locked the doors and allowed cobwebs and ivy to creep over the warehouse, tucked away in the darkest corner of the studio lot. The children of Paramount actors, roaming the sets of *An Officer and a Gentleman* and *Star Trek II: The Wrath of Khan*, learned to fear the tale of the strange old woman, now reduced to a mere rumour, little more than the words of a song to skip along to:

Old Maggie
Lost her eye
No one wants her apple pie

Old Maggie
On the street
Jeepy-creepy backwards feet!

Time passed, and the garden overgrew. 'A baseball landing on Maggie's roof was a lost ball,' as the saying went.

And then, one day in 1993, hope finally arrived in old Maggie's life. I won't go into the story of the day the set designer of *Friends* found the old lot, like a lost Aladdin's cave of design treasures, and immediately moved the cast and crew in to begin filming. Suffice it to say that over the next decade, Margaret finally found what she had been looking for in life. Peeping out from hidden cupboards, light fittings and the bathroom we never see on screen, some say it is Margaret's voice that rose above all the others during filming; that whooped with joy at Ross and Rachel's first kiss, and cried when they were on a break; who laughed loudest at Joey's hunger pangs and sighed for Phoebe's songs. Some say Maggie is there now still, behind that closed door; happier now, and old, so old, peeping through the spyhole, waiting for another friend to come.

MARY-BETH GARDENER, MASSACHUSETTS

What do blind people see in their dreams?

Terence Trent, Derbyshire

Naturally, this depends on how long the person has been blind; those who experienced sight as a child retain visual dreams, whereas someone who has been blind from birth has dreams that rely entirely on the senses of taste, touch, smell and hearing.

Far more interesting to we cognitive psychologists is the question of *visual* language; what deaf people 'see' in their heads when thinking of something to say, or when dreaming about a conversation. Oxford Professor of Advanced Cognition Rupert Delaney, who happens to have been deaf since birth, wrote a wonderfully spiky article in the *Times Educational Supplement* on just this subject, reserving a tremendous amount of vitriol for the 'wall-eyed, dough-faced succubus' who for many years signed for the deaf on Sunday morning television.

According to Delaney, over years of watching *See, Hear*, the unfortunate woman – always there at the bottom of the screen, gesticulating away – began to infest every waking moment of his being. Even the simplest private thought – God, this conference is boring, and, I could really do with a wee, are the examples Delaney gives – would be visually articulated in his mind as the jiggling of chubby arms and 'shit-eating grin' of the BBC signer. Summoning up the courage to propose to his ex-wife over a candlelit dinner, searching for the right words to say: all dissolved into a

109

confused cerebral mush of fat, flapping hands and a tired permanent wave. Even Delaney's nights were not his own, every cry of sexual pleasure, every character of his dreams, 'each and every sentence of my life visualised in the person of that godforsaken woman, speaking the tongues of men in a beige Marks and Spencer cardigan'.

Delaney's article famously led to the woman asking him out to lunch, where the most remarkable thing happened. Delaney, so famous for his waspish criticism and huge ego, so truly, terribly awful to his nemesis in print, was in fact utterly seduced by meeting her in person – as if his own thoughts and language and consciousness had been made flesh, staring back at him over the fish course. A rival psychologist wrily commented that it was almost as if the woman, for so long the vehicle through which Delaney was able to articulate his conscious mind, *was the physical embodiment of his ego*. Freud would have had a field day with that one.

DR MICHAEL GEORGE, ONLINE UNIVERSITY OF CAMBRIDGE,

CORNWALL

Royal Antarctic Expedition

Dearest Marjory,

Progress! The embarrassment of the Reform Club leaving party and the attack of the omnibus is behind us, and we are making good time with our preparations for the voyage south. Baines is our nominated quartermaster; he has a fine head for figures and is well on the way to correcting our early mistakes, whereby the grain, chickens and huskies were all kept in the same compartment of the dry dock in Wapping. Baines has instead developed an ingenious plan 'B': the ship — our dear HMS Bugle — will sail to the Antarctic carrying only the grain; then return empty to our fair shores for the chickens — wait, no, the dogs would have eaten the chickens during the outward voyage of the grain. Anyway, after months hard at work on a logical solution, Baines assures me he has this covered, mathematically speaking, and that we shall be able to begin the actual exploration in around five years' time: the summer of 1914 would be perfect for such frippery, fun and derring-do, wouldn't you agree?

Until then, we can but uncork another bottle of fine Madeira, and wait. I think of you often, Marjory, and the children. How Tarquin and Millie must have grown! And although I know that you are all only on the other side of St James's Park waiting for me, rest easy that I am well fed here at the club, and that I will uphold your honour by reaching the Pole before that blasted boor Scott or that young flash-heart Shackleton.

Must dash, my love — Wilson has promised a spot of climbing practice and we propose to make it up the grand staircase of the club in time for tiffin. Onward!

I remain, as ever, your affectionate,

Phozzy

(Letter postmarked, 26 January 1910 second class. Arrived Monday.)

W hat happens to the second-class post to make it arrive more slowly? Surely it goes through the same systems as the first-class post?

Dorothy Yes, Great Yarmouth

You would think so, wouldn't you? But here's how it really works: picture a lovely factory, with beautifully oiled conveyor belts whizzing perfect packages into jolly red vans, their engines already running to deliver your post. Now forget that, and imagine lots of busy mice dressed in tiny blue uniforms, smoking pipes and pottering about with huge envelopes on their backs marked 'Second Class'. Forget that, too – I just liked the idea and might put it to my superiors. Now picture your unloved second-class letter dropping into the bright red postbox at the end of your street, which is what *actually* happens. The slot on the right – 'First Class and International' – leads into the box, which is emptied every day between 10.30 a.m. and 5 p.m. The second slot – 'Second Class' – in fact leads directly into the public sewer system. While the first-class post speeds on its way to being delivered within a matter of days, then, I'm afraid we just have to sit back and wait for the sewer to empty into the nearest river and drift downstream into HM's Postal Nets. You might think it's a pretty stupid sort of system, but over the last 150 years it's

112

proved to be an effective way of ensuring that we can deliver it to you a) late and b) in a sorry state. Which is probably all you deserve for trying to save ten pence.

TERENCE DIAERESIS-UMLAUT, HM POSTAL HEADQUARTERS,

BATTERSEA SEWAGE WORKS

Is it true that there are only eleven basic plots in literature and film, and that no matter how inventive a writer tries to be, their work will never be original?

Caroline Pigg, Telford

I'm afraid it is true. If you look hard enough, the eleven basic themes are there in any book or film you care to mention: a case of revenge, the return of the prodigal son, the doomed love triangle . . . No matter how hard directors try to disguise the fact, the 'golden eleven' are always there in the background, strangling originality and creativity in its cradle. There's clearly little difference in character motivation, narrative arc and theme, for instance, between Preston Sturges's *Sullivan's Travels*, Michelangelo Antonioni's *Zabriskie Point* and Shannon Tweed's late masterwork, *Secret Unlawful Entry VI*.

PADRAIG O'MURRAY, *PADRAIG O'MURRAY FILM GUIDE*

I don't agree with Mr O'Murray. Speaking for myself, I read your letter with real excitement, Caroline. After many months wasted in the development of what I thought to be an entirely new colour, your question piqued my interest and fired my enthusiasm all over again, and I immediately began furiously cutting and pasting literary genres together, looking for a whole new way of storytelling. By mixing the heat and passion and energy of 'bonkbusters' with the mystery and noirish atmosphere of 'crime' fiction, I have come up with a recipe for bestsellerdom I call 'sex crime'. Perhaps the *Old Git* would like to print an extract from my next novel, *Private Dicks*, in the next issue?

SIMON SAYERS, COUNTY DURHAM

Corrections & Clarfications

Our sports correspondent writes:

We would like to apologise for any confusion caused by our report on the one-day cricket match between Surrey and Glamorgan, where we recorded Surrey's score as 11,741. Obviously in a fifty-over game the maximum score is 1800, which would involve a six being hit from every ball. You could conceivably add a couple of hundred for potential wides and other no-balls, but no more as any higher number would prevent the game's conclusion owing to the delay incurred. The correct score for Surrey in the match was in fact 11,740 for 9.

W hy do we say that people who are
enjoying themselves are having 'a whale
of a time'?

Tim Muggeridge, Suffolk

This is because whales, which are remarkably sophisticated
creatures with complex social rules and modes of behaviour,
have done away with the polite fiction that size doesn't
matter. The lead male in any pod gains his position not
from his strength or speed at swimming, but from the size
of his endowment. The average blue whale's 'member' is
nine feet long, but some have been recorded as long as
twenty-three feet, and with a girth that would, if hollowed
out, form a tunnel wide enough to admit an automated
wheelchair (a useful fact if you ever have to hide a
wheelchair in a hurry and a hollowed out whale's cock is to
hand). Many examples are on display in the American
Whale Museum, in Washington – it's on the floor beneath
the headquarters of the American Feminist Society and at
lunchtime many of those women can be seen walking to
and fro, tucking into their beef sandwiches. Cold-blooded
or not, whales are highly sexed creatures and female whales
select a mate according to whether he is able to locate the
W-spot, an area within the female's sexual organs where a
gathering of nerve endings form a patch of hyper-sexual-

sensitivity which if caressed is guaranteed to provoke orgasm.

The male whales are helped by the fact that this spot is about the size of an archery target or a large truck's wheel. Thus, the rutting whale, if he is so lucky as to be chosen, can spend his adult life almost permanently in heat, which accounts for the common sightings of whale spouts by humans. Whales in fact breathe very gently and slowly except in moments of sexual release, when the great spouting of air and sea froth is the equivalent of a post-coital gasp. So, as the Inuits and several coastal American aboriginal tribes surmised, it would be the dream of many a man or woman to have 'a whale of a time'.

APRIL LANDING, APRIL LANDING INSTITUTE OF SEXUAL
FURTHERANCE, KENSTBURG, WYOMING

Not so. Most lexicographers attribute the remark confidently to George Bernard Shaw, the Irish wit, playwright and Nobel Prize-winning vegetarian.

The end of the nineteenth century was, of course, famous for its debauchery – the term *'fin de siècle'* is now a byword for dandyism and social excess – and no man was better known as a thrower of memorable parties than Captain Andrew 'Titus' Kidd, the great whaling entrepreneur without whom, it was said, 'no man might light his oil lamp at night nor step outside by day, for want of brilliantine in his hair'. Quite simply, Jay Gatsby had nothing on old Kidd. Best remembered is his 1887 'party of a century' – for which Gershwin wrote a song that most people know from Prince's cover version: 'By God and Queen we'll party as if twere 1899'. The evening took place in the Valley of the Kings, near Luxor, and involved the construction of an entire palace of ice. Guests were ordered to strip throughout the day in time to the slow melting of the walls in the hot Egyptian sun (a scene immortalised by Ayn Rand in her 1957 novel *Atlas Shrugged*), while a forty-foot-high fountain in the shape of a whale spurted jets of molten Belgian chocolate on the cavorting throng. The reserved Kidd himself remained aloof from the saturnalia, birdspotting from a nearby hill in plus-fours and a pith helmet.

At that time merely the arts critic of the *Star*, writing under the name Corno di Basseto, Shaw wrote of the event: 'The grandiosity of Kidd's parties truly matches that of the beasts in pursuit of which he has made his name. A whale of a party indeed, a veritable kraken of excess that should make a Pharaoh blush'. It may be noted that, for all his apparent disapproval, Shaw went on to become one of Kidd's regular and most celebrated guests; and while the playwright is known for his Shavian comeback, 'Yes, but what if the child were to have your brain and my looks?', it is less well known that when he said it, he was covered in chocolate, wearing nothing more than sock suspenders and a top hat.

DR ROLAND VIGOUR, LUTON AIRPORT PARKWAY

W hy are great lesbian writers not just called great writers?

Solange Esprit, Lyons

Well, Miss Esprit, I know what you mean; Philip Roth is never referred to as 'a great old, white writer who likes a bit of slap and tickle', but I see that as an opportunity missed. Where's the harm in finding out a bit more about the person behind the name? You will be pleased to know that I have started up my own publishing company, where I will be actively promoting the sexual proclivities of my writers. Already signed up is the shy, naughty crime writer Marsha Crowe; the constantly masturbating medievalist Derek Trentchon (do look out for his forthcoming memoir, *Feeling Myself Again*); and Nobel Laureate Vakla Pestenc, who loves it up the bum. Do check out our website, if your firewall will allow it through.

DONALD EFFERSON, PUBLISHING DIRECTOR,
GUTTER PRESS

W hat would happen if a cat and a dog did it?

Brandon Carmichael, Garelochhead, Scotland

Cats and dogs act as such mortal enemies that it seems they're thriving off some kind of sexual tension – much like, say, Arsenal and Spurs fans on the day of a north London derby. Yet it isn't so – no matter how many perverted scientists look into the matter, it seems that they just hate each other.

But other different species have not proved so incompatible. It has been found, for instance, that a crocodile can have sex with a koala, and that the resulting amphibian offspring prefers to hug the trees although, unlike its fully koala sister creatures, when it gets off its tits on eucalyptus and falls out of the branches into rivers, it can swim to safety.

Other bizarre cross-breedings have occurred, such as the weird creature born to a giraffe in Africa in 1974. Fat and stumpy, with a long, spiral-shaped neck, the geneticist who tested its DNA announced to an amazed press that its father must have been 'the best endowed pig that there ever was'.

But weirdest of all were the experiments that were said to have been carried out at a rogue American laboratory in the 1940s, when human women were allegedly paid to consort with simians of different breeds, to see if pregnancy could ensue. Although all findings were eradicated in a fire in 2001, there are whispers that the experiments succeeded and that some of the resultant children are still at large today in US society. The laboratory and its archive were scrapped suspiciously soon after George W. Bush came to power and the fire broke out a couple of days later. Whenever I see him on the telly, I always wonder . . . What do you think? I reckon, orang-utan.

HARLEY MASON, ALBUQUERQUE

I don't understand why this question is hypothetical. My cats and dogs have been doing it for years, and ours is a very happy household, thank you very much. If any *Old Git* readers are interested in buying a cog, Gerald and I have a lovely litter of marmalade Rottweiler/Siamese cross pittens at the moment. It took us years to work out how to make it happen, but after Gerald managed to build a set of comfortable stilts for Felix the Siamese from an old Airfix kit of a Lancaster bomber, we were well away!

VALERIE PARSNIP, BRIGHTON

Can any Buddhist tell me: what is the sound of one hand clapping?

'Big' Suze Little, Brown University

My grandfather, Michiko Kamasura, devoted his whole life to answering this question. Michiko-san was a humble man, a Zen Buddhist monk who, from the age of six, lived up in the mountains of Nakura province, in the north of Hokkaido. As the first cherry blossom of spring bloomed, young Michiko would sit in the monastery's gravel garden, pondering the Buddha's question. What is the sound of one hand clapping? Spring turned to the heat and humidity of summer; summer turned to autumn and still my grandfather would sit, calmly surveying the regular lines of raked gravel and the gentle, lonely drift of a leaf from the garden's cherry tree. Years passed. As Michiko grew older he began to see patterns in the garden; the cycle of the natural year echoed in the graceful arc of the raked lines and of the human hands that made them. Hands. Now an old man and the last of his order, my grandfather rose stiffly, regarded his own hands, made his way purposefully over to his beloved cherry tree as the first snowflake of winter fell – and stood on a rake, which smacked him in the face. I wish I'd been there; *Mr Bean Goes Abroad* was still fifty years in the future, so even if old Michiko didn't find the key to enlightenment, he still stumbled across a small piece of comedy gold.

KOJO KAMASURA, KYOTO

It is silence.
It is the silence of the universe. The silence of God. The silence of the Himalayan mountains tempered only by the whispering of ghostly winds, which might be the spirits of a thousand dead strangers, or a million restless souls.

N. COGNITO, TIBET

[It's me again, Penny, your old editor. I wish you peace in your heart and soul. Although communication with the outside world is prohibited here in the monastery, I am smuggling this scroll out via Armal, a sympathetic servant who served with the British Army until 1947 and now works up and down these mountains even though he's in his ninetieth year (would that I had such abs at his age!). I came ashore from my stowaway position on what I thought was a harmless anchovy trawler but which was raided in

121

international waters by DEA agents. In the mélée I
managed to jump ship and paddled twelve miles to the coast
using an airtight sac of brownish powder (what was this?
Illegal pepper smuggling?) which I sold to a hysterical
bunch of dockers in Goa for what seemed rather a large
sum. That was enough to get me to the foothills of the
Himalayas where I fell under the spell of Buddha and made
pilgrimage towards my current location, a shrine and
monastery in Chinese-held Tibet. Can't argue with the
views, and the diet is extraordinarily good for one, not to
mention the hill-climbing! But it's the philosophy of my
teachers that makes me feel reborn. I feel no fear of
anything, no anger, not even to that bane of my former life,
the offensive cretin Plum. The universe is like a clear,
streaming body of water and I am but one particle in it. I
understand that now. Yet, this epiphany reached, I seek to
return to civilisation to spread the word. Plus it's nearly a
year since I ate a full English breakfast, and I miss the
black pud. And there's been no pornography to speak of for
my last eight thousand miles aside from the local 'She's only
wearing three layers of clothing!' type that Indians like. Yet
the kung fu-trained monks will not hear of me leaving, as
conversion demands life-long silence. But you know me,
Penny, I'm a wily one! I've fashioned a rope from the braids
of my chest hair and shall abseil to freedom once Armal
returns with my fare for the train to Delhi. You'll tap petty
cash for that for me, and send it to this address, won't you,
Penny, my dear, dear Penny? Or all you'll hear from me is
the sound of one hand clapping . . .]

Why is it that, no matter how carefully I tuck them away, electrical cables around the house always seem to become hopelessly tangled?

Rita Knowles, Adelaide

Put simply for a non-scientist reader: latent electromagnetic fields that linger after turning off an electrical device bend and curl the cables; and for an appliance that is used every day, such as a television, even a week is sufficient time to curl everything up into a maddening mess. Infuriating for you and I, but imagine how the technicians who work on Even Deeper Blue, the world's biggest super-computer, must feel. Housed in the world's largest building in the Nevada desert (bigger even than the Nazi-built Tempelhof airport terminal in Berlin), Even Deeper Blue requires some 70,000,000 miles of cable, which twists and coils and tangles its way through hundreds of acres of floor space. Indeed, as reported in the *Nevada Sun* newspaper, EDB almost never made it to its famous chess match with Gary Kasparov in 1997. An explosion in the neighbouring Japanese food warehouse sent seventeen tonnes of egg noodles smashing through the roof of EDB enterprises – which in turn tempted an estimated hundred thousand rattlesnakes out of the surrounding desert to feed and writhe and mate. So spare a thought for those less fortunate than you, the next time you take your iPod out of your pocket and spend an angry moment untangling the earphones.

CHIP FEEDLE, PHOENIX, ARIZONA

[Molly – Marc here. Send this weekly podcast out for the Young and Old Gits, yeah? Thanks, mate. Try to make sure the Old Gits don't publish a transcript this time, though! 'Hey guys! Who's in the house? That's absolutely 110 per cent right: Marc is. I really hope you're all settling in. The cleaners have asked me if you could use the toilets from now on, and we need to respect those guys; I know there's a tradition of "going" in the window boxes to help the pansies, but think health and safety, yeah? Would you sit on the window and wee outwards at home? Also, could all staff please copy-check their publications before they go to print? I'm a reasonable guy but our readers are valued, cocksmoking titboxes; someone's been adding swearwords to my fucking podcasts and printing them in the Old Git, *and it reflects really badly on what we're trying to do here! Nightmare! Peace, Marc.']*

W here are the snows of yesteryear?

A. Prophet, address unknown

They have fallen upon the Holy Land, covering it in a white blanket and making it invisible. But lightning will strike the Holy Land and burn off the snow so that it may stand again in its former glory, when the hawk and the falcon unite and swoop.

THE HYENA, ADDRESS UNKNOWN

Yeah, you say that, Kev, but the hawk has to actually be able to get hold of his thunder, right? That bloke in Vauxhall you put me in touch with sold me three pounds of fucking *plasticine*, not Semtex as you promised. (Actually it was quite fun because I made figurines of all the judges on *X-Factor* and I'm going to present it as part of my coursework for my art & design NVQ.) Maybe the falcon had better luck, but the Holy Land seems pretty frozen over from where I'm sitting.

THE HAWK, KENNINGTON

Thing is, I was halfway through making these 'home-made explosives' that you told us to find out about on the internet, and I had all the ingredients out on our lounge floor – the compost, bicarbonate of soda and everything, and me mum came home quicker than I thought from Morrisons. She flipped out when she saw all this crap everywhere so I had to explain that I was mixing a special compost for her pot plants. Then she stood over me as I repotted all of them, one by one. I swear, I'm living in fear, man. Every time she goes back for a bay leaf or a sprig of

125

rosemary I break out in a sweat – one knocked over pot and this whole house could go up. Cheers, Kev – sorry, Hyena – nice one.

THE FALCON, BATTERSEA

Patience, my friends, patience. I shall be in touch again with new instructions, and the mouth of God will deliver the righteous message to the decadent peoples of this blasphemous land, and the snows of yesteryear will thaw. Right, type that up, Gary, will you, lad. I don't know, who'd organise a terrorist cell. Bloody cretins. I blame the parents. Oh, and if you're going out to the post office I'll have a packet of panatellas and some tonic water. Slimline, mind. Had to mix my bath-time gin with *Ribena* last night for want of anything better.

THE HYENA, ADDRESS UNKNOWN

Why does sick always contain diced carrot, even when you haven't eaten it?

Margaret Bircher, Dinedor, Herefordshire

This is a question that has dumbfounded biologists since carrots were first diced (you'd expect me here to say *when* carrots were first diced, but we can't be sure there ever was a time that they *weren't* diced), which was as early as seventh-century Wales, at least. Certainly this is when Saint Llwywd, confronted by many of his followers throwing up during an epic thirty-day crossing of the Brecon Beacons, began his series of sixteen Parables of the Carrot. Translated from the Welsh into plain English prose, this neglected part of Dark Ages apocrypha includes: 'Consider the dice of carrot, swallowed by life, resolute in the dark times and when he is called, rising up to the light of God's embrace'. Llwywd's followers, however, found a better explanation in the figure of his cook, a stumpy, eccentric Viking albino he had met in a mead hall, and who they discreetly murdered, explaining that he had run away. The Saint's theorising on the carrot stopped immediately, and he moved to more profound phenomena on which to reflect, such as leeks.

Leonardo, too, commented in his notebooks on the resilience of diced carrots. Finding a hundred-year-old man in a local hospital, the anatomy-obsessed Renaissance man waited gleefully for the man's death so he could prove his theory right. He had assurances from the centenarian that he had not eaten any diced carrot since his Tuscan childhood eighty-seven years before. On the old man's death and dissection, therefore, Leonardo was jubilant to find cubes of the red vegetable still present in the stomach. He posited, in a sequence of thirty drawings and accompanying notes, that diced carrot was one of the lightest and strongest materials in nature, and designed a series of machines and devices that might be constructed from it. The series culminated in a spectacular flying machine twice as large as the later and more famous model that is now displayed to the public at Clos Lucé, Leonardo's home in France. With the second, smaller one he was forced to resort to wood, canvas and rope, after the greengrocers of Florence proved unequal to his demands.

YORICK BELLING, KANDAHAR

Who cares? After much trial and error, I've discovered that, by eating small pieces of multi-coloured Lego and relying on the phantom carrots to provide the straight-sided pieces of orange, I can now puke up a completed Rubik's Cube on demand. *Britain's Got Talent*, here I come!

DIGBY CRIMP, AGED SEVENTEEN, MARLOWE

My mum used to threaten, 'Don't pull faces – if the wind changes you'll stay that way!' Has this ever happened?

Christa Pachyderm, Missouri

I never believed this when my mother used to say it, and enjoyed making grotesque faces whenever her back was turned. That was before my Uncle Roderick returned from the war, however, horribly scarred with shrapnel wounds. He stayed with us while he recuperated from his injuries, but he was unfortunately so ugly that the local children used to gather round the house hoping for a look at him and would then run off screaming when he appeared. One day, though, when a larger group than usual assembled while he was smoking a cigarette in the yard, he decided to play along and turned around attempting the most horrible grimace he could twist his face into.

At that exact moment a huge prairie wind blew, strong enough to knock down the fence and blow some of the trees over. It swept him off his feet and threw him against the barn, fifty feet away at the back of the garden. When the wind had died down the whole family rushed to see if he was okay, but something extraordinary had happened. It was later explained by a doctor that a muscle had snapped in his cheek, but in his attempt to writhe his features into a gargoyle's grimace he had accidentally made himself appear ruggedly handsome, and that's how his face remained.

He was soon on his feet again and took up his pre-war job, which was playing jazz piano, with renewed gusto, eventually touring the US playing for Frank Sinatra. With his new face he was quite the swordsman and is said to have fathered dozens of illegitimate children before his fatal heart attack while in bed with Miss Montana, fifteen years later.

LOTTE CREEDY, GLASSVILLE, KANSAS

What's the riskiest game of Risk ever played?

Joan Cooker, Krakow

History has not looked favourably on Richard Nixon up to now. His reputation will fall even further, however, if certain revelations from the famous 'expletive deleted' tapes are ever confirmed. One of the most scandalous of these is that, permanently unsure how to act over the Vietnam debacle he had inherited from LBJ, he took to playing the boardgame Risk to determine American strategy in the war, challenging almost anyone who stepped into the Oval Office to see if they could beat him. Apparently he commissioned a new version of the game that took place exclusively over the territories of Vietnam, Cambodia and Laos.

Unfortunately for American troops (and countless South-east Asian civilians), however, he was dreadful at it and lost every time. He became so obsessed with the game itself that he forgot the war was still going on, and eventually organised for the Democratic National Committee headquarters (housed in the Watergate complex) to be burgled so that he might learn some of the secret strategies of his chief rivals. (Henry Kissinger drove Nixon to distraction by always winning without appearing to make any effort at all, but this was because he had established an intricate network of cameras and spies to help him cheat. He formulated his foreign policy – for which, after multiple years-long campaigns of deception, overthrown democracy and mass death, he was awarded the Nobel Peace Prize – not by playing Risk, but blind man's bluff.)

Should readers fear that similar tactics have been employed over the recent mess in Iraq, they should consider that Risk is far too complex for George W. Bush to comprehend. If a recently fired White House aide is to be believed, the president relaxes by playing snap, pooh sticks and the popular game Britney's Dance Beat for Playstation 2.

GENE B. MCWILDE, CO. DONEGAL.

It is not just Vietnam that was determined by a board game. The Crimean War was not truly fought over trade routes to the subcontinent, but was in effect an international manifestation of an ongoing squabble between Queen Victoria and Tsar Nicholas I over a disputed hand of rummy.

Similarly, the War of Jenkins's Ear was in fact an escalation of a dispute over the outcome of a game of badminton, where the English and Spanish players could not agree whether the shuttlecock was out of play after it got wedged in the side of Jenkins's head.

BRADLEY HOLLICE, TEWKESBURY

How stupid is bungee jumping?

Billy Braithwaite, aged eight, Sunderland

As a former professional soldier and keen bungee jumper, I would say this: if one remembers to attach the cord to one's legs before jumping, there are relatively few risks involved. Nobody told that to poor old Smithers, though. Game chap, Smithers. A foot shorter than he was and he'll never walk again, but an absolute brick under fire.

BRIGADIER SIR MICHAEL BEEZEWATER, SURREY

Royal Antarctic Expedition

Dearest Marjory,

After so many false starts, a man would be forgiven, I should suppose, for basking somewhat in the glory of standing all but alone on the very fundament of the world. Trekking for many months across ice and snow, manhauling over crevasses and knotted sastrugi alike with only Baines, Pemberton and some penguins for company, such a man might think, in fact, that he had finally 'made it' in life.

Sadly, I am not that man, Marjory. I can't think of anything worse. I'm afraid I never made it out of Portsmouth harbour, where I met a rugged stevedore named Briggs down at the docks, with whom I believe I have fallen in love. Briggs has a face like a blind cobbler's thumb but he has a good heart and forearms to die for. Forgive me, Marjory; I leave everything to you and the children, of course: and although I suppose I will never be a famous explorer now that I shall be cooking and cleaning for Briggs full time, I hope that one day Tarquin might take up the family banner and make a go of it. Oh Christ, must go — I've left the oven on,
Respectfully yours,
Phozzy

(Letter postmarked 30 March 1911, second class received Friday.)

Is there really nothing to fear but fear itself? Fear of what?

Simon Fry, Clapham

I was interested to read Mr Fry's irresponsibly jaunty posting, since I consider myself the country's leading specialist in treating phobophobes – sad, lonely individuals trapped by their fear of crashing bores who bang on about their fear of spiders, heights or celery. Freud himself writes of a celebrated case – one 'Frau K' – who was veritably consumed by agoraphobophobia: an irrational fear of those who fear the outside world. Since all agoraphobics are confined indoors by their condition, Frau K was forced to walk the streets in order to avoid them. There, however, given her obsession with the condition, she found herself consorting frequently with claustrophobes, who she found to be personally much more objectionable than agoraphobes. Indeed, she took a deep dislike to anyone who enjoyed the outdoors. Such a tiny comfort zone did this leave her that when Freud returned from his 'research' trip down the dark alleys of Biarritz in 1906, he found her obsessed with not leaving the narrow space of a doorway.

'Why are you trying to block me out?' he asked.

'I'm not!' she cried.

'No, seriously, I need to get in, I need a shit,' he replied.

She died of exposure in the harsh winter of 1934, tragically; though dark rumours persist in the psychoanalytical community that the 'exposure' in question occurred in Dr Freud's private hot tub, under hypnosis.

DR PERCIVAL COCKING, BERKSHIRE

D'you know what, there really *are* situations that are worth being afraid of. I used to be terribly fearful and timid until I attended the 'self-enhancement, validation and fear disposal' course at the April Landing Institute of Personal Development in the late eighties (before April got with her own personal trainer and moved into Sexual Furtherance). This taught me valuably to identify fear and ignore it, and I came top of my graduating class, where we each placed our fears in a box and tossed them in the Pacific Ocean. A few months later I found myself in a car driven by my paranoid-schizophrenic cousin Mandy who was trying to drive us off a cliff. Calmly I identified my fear and pacified it, then tried to talk Mandy out of killing us both. It didn't work – we crashed over the edge, she died and I lost a leg.

On holiday in Australia the following summer, a poisonous snake slithered on to the path ahead of me. Again, I remained calm as though nothing was happening, and carried on walking, whistling happily to myself, even after it bit me on the wrist, until, after crawling seventeen miles to the nearest motorway, I passed out. When I woke my arm had been amputated. My flight home went via London and when I introduced myself to the guy in the next seat, and he replied, 'Richard Reid, shoe bomber. Charmed,' I decided it was time to start being frightened again.

NORVILLE AGATE, SOUTH CAROLINA

If there's nothing to fear but fear itself, are stress-related deaths partly due to our continually being told we're too stressed?

Gary Bastille, Lisbon

A point well made! This is the great unspoken-about killer in our country, Gary. In fact, after heart disease, lung cancer and stress, being told about stress is our fourth largest life-taker. The fact that most people leading stressful lives do not choose to lead them and can't change anything about them, is not relieved by being told that stress is a killer. Of course, it adds to the problem. Indeed, in societies where millions of people are stressed but the deleterious effects are not so widely reported, such as Japan, deaths from stress are much lower. Similar figures are reported with heart attacks, as it has been proven that people afraid of heart attacks are much more likely to have them, especially if every time they switch on the TV news or open a magazine they have HEART ATTACK screaming at them.

No wonder the monks of Mount Athos have been hailed as the healthiest collective in the world: they might eat well, but they don't get the newspaper, and they have no TV.

JOHN GARSTANG, WIMBLEDON

If God is dead, what else do we have to cling on to?

Sappho Regale, Celebration, Florida

I'm afraid there isn't much left to hold on to, Sappho. With Marx, Freud and Judaeo-Christianity all reeling from criticism on all sides, none of our idols are safe. Following the success of *The God Delusion*, Richard Dawkins is reported to be about to publish *I Don't Like it, Not One Bit* – a damning, thrillingly systematic dismantling of modern magic and everything Paul Daniels has ever stood for. Christopher Hitchens is said to be working on *Lorraine Kelly on the Ducking Stool*, and with daytime television out of the way the only thing that remains is to prove that Victoria Beckham simply does not exist. It is a cold, bleak world out there, Sappho.

THOMAS CROAKER, FABIAN APPRECIATION SOCIETY, LONDON

Freud's teachings are not dead, Thomas. We still have much to learn from the great man. One of my own patients, Max J, is a better person for the work we have done together on the couch over the last few years. Max's case is an interesting one: since childhood, he had been plagued by a recurring dream whereby he killed his father by stabbing him, after being discovered sleeping with his own mother. It took many hypnosis sessions to get to the bottom of the matter. Eventually, it became clear to me that the patient was simply repressing an upsetting childhood memory whereby he had accidentally sat on a cucumber, repeatedly, while hiding in the dark, warm, wet larder under the stairs. Could you have solved that case without Freud, Thomas? I think not.

SAMANTHA KRONK MD, BERLIN

Why me?

Charlotte Cocksmut, Tewkesbury

Why not you, Charlotte? You're a woman, with feelings and needs and legs and a back. You have got legs, haven't you? Oh dear, I'm always putting my foot in it, making assumptions. Oh dear – I mean, I hope you can put your foot – any foot – in something too. Anyway, yes, you have needs; we all have needs. I once sat on a vacuum cleaner pipe and turned it on. I didn't *need* to – I just did it. And as they wheeled me – well, wheeled the vacuum cleaner with me sitting on it – into casualty, I remember thinking, Why me? too. But it *did* feel jolly nice before it got stuck. Anyway, I just thought I'd write in to say: hang in there, Charlotte!

MARJORIE RAINING, IPSWICH

Hey, Charlotte, that's an unusual surname, isn't it? But it's your family name, I assume, not one you made up? And as with all rude-sounding names (like 'Bottoms', meaning a family that lived in the bottom of a valley), it has a simple explanation: 'cock' is a vocal derivative of 'coke', meaning coal, and 'smut' means ash. So Cocksmut means coal ash, because your forebears once lived near one of Britain's key factory districts, right? If not, give me a ring, you filthy bitch.

ZORIN LOBERUNGER, HARLEY, IOWA

[Ed note: Dear Penelope, I am sorry that these made it into the magazine. I know how sensitive you are about the loss of your mother's legs. People leave all sorts of things on buses and get them back again. Besides, who'd find a use for a double set of prosthetics? They must serve a superior brand of gin at those bingo nights if she crawled home without noticing. Let me know if there's anything I can do – there are some old crutches I found at the back of the office I'd be glad to be rid of. Really glad – they stink of death. While I'm on the topic, can you get Consuela to spray those upper *shelves with disinfectant? Or, better, weedkiller? Those things overhanging the pot plants look like death cap mushrooms. I'm determined that we get this place spick and span in case of one of Marc's health and safety checks. The most casual inspection would close us down – and quite rightly!]*

Do arseholes have ants?

Emma Young, London

The questioner presumably finds such an outlandish notion to be in some way risible. Perhaps she would feel differently if she, like I, had returned home one evening to find her husband bending her teenage Latvian au pair over the family formicarium. The answer to your question, then, is 'yes', his name is Malcolm and I hope his balls drop off.

MRS MALCOLM FEATHERSTONEHAUGH, BERKSHIRE

140

Is there any language in the world that has a specific word for that feeling when you wipe your bum too hard?

Jamie Coleman, London

There is indeed, Jamie – though it is not clear from your question whether you are referring to wiping your bum too hard *once* after having moved one's bowels – what doctors call a 'rectal ablution' – or wiping your bum repeatedly and vigorously against the erect member of another man in a public toilet – what I would call 'bum sex'. Either way, the Tuareg people of the Saharan desert do have a word that sums up the first interpretation: *'Al-maqua'har!!'* This untranslatable exclamation of astonished anguish has less to do with the singular nomadic culture of the Tuareg way of life, and more to do with the sensation of wiping one's arse with toilet paper covered in rough Saharan sand. *Al-maqua'har!!*

STEFAN MOREAU, UNIVERSITY OF GENEVA

If I fell down a disused mineshaft, would Lassie really run and get help; or just sit there licking his balls?

Brad Shunt, Wyoming

141

I'm fairly sure that Lassie was a girl, Brad. Sorry to be a stickler for detail! You must think me a dreadful blue-stockinged bore. Anyway, to rephrase your question: would Lassie really run and get help; or just sit there licking her minge?

VENETIA COPPER, HAMPTON WICK

I enjoyed earlier answers to this question – especially the one from Phil McGee about how his dog, Pickles, rescued him from a searingly bad acid trip by literally licking his master's balls. That made me laugh. But I was really writing because of an interesting piece in our local newspaper earlier this year, where a local dog fell into a mineshaft, and badly broke his legs. The dog's owner was a lovely bloke called Lah Si, a popular member of Malmaston's Malaysian community, and he immediately ran off to a nearby farmhouse, waving and crying out in Malaysian for someone to fetch help. Eventually, the locals realised that he was trying to tell them something, and followed him to where the dog was in trouble.

Quite a heartwarming story, really – but it turns out the whole thing was filmed by Malaysian TV; apparently, Lah Si is something of a star over there, and every week his dog ends up clogging the wheels of an industrial tractor, or falling down a well while his master gets help. Weird, eh?

MIKE FREIGHT, MALMASTON, DERBYSHIRE

How come fast food stores only seem to employ people with bad acne?

Lorraine 'Quiche' Lorraine, Idaho

On the contrary, my friend. Here at the BURGER BELIEF! chain we employ people with only the finest acne to be found. The average interviewee is not allowed through the door unless they have at least six volcanic pimples on their face and these are then tested with extremely sensitive and expensive tools for width, depth and visibility. The ability to communicate, or fulfil orders within, say, a half hour, are deemed irrelevant (any dickhead can serve fried-cow's-asshole-in-a-bap), which is why our parent company has proudly renamed itself Acme Acne (formerly Haliburton Corp).

GULF HANES, SAN ANTONIO, TEXAS

Ever since I started working in the local burger joint, people have given me shit for being covered in zits. Well, I've just joined up all of the pimples on my face, and it spells out 'COCK'. Do you want fries with that?

CHIP BUNKT, MISSOURI

How did Tooting Bec in South London come to be so named?

Arnold Sote, Wandsworth

The name Tooting came about when Henry I rode through the place and was heard by his knights to be tutting at what he saw. It had become a haven for 'disreputable ladies' who had been cast out by the disdainful residents of Balham (then called 'Bell End'), and who had set up home down the road. Good old British snobbery soon established itself even there, resulting in the split between Tutting village and its even more notorious cousin, the Tutting Broad Way. The Bec part came nearly a hundred years later from Richard the Lionheart, whose mistress Bess lived there. As he walked around the castle of Chalus-Chabrol in Northern France a knight asked Richard which part of England he missed the most. He got halfway through saying, 'Tooting, because——' when the fatal arrow struck him in the shoulder.

SAM O. BINE, BARNSLEY

I once knew a 'Tooting Bec'. I don't know how she reached such a low range of notes. A diet of pulses and a bucket to amplify the sound, I suppose.

MR PLUM, PLUMSTEAD

Mr Plum's response is, I fear, in jest. Of course Tooting Bec was the name of the fictionalised romantic interest for Spring Heeled Jack, in the many myths and stories spread about that person in the penny dreadfuls of the Victorian era. First reported in the 1830s, Jack was supposed to be a creature with diabolical features and a gentleman's bearing who would leap out and attack people at night before escaping by jumping up on to roofs or over high walls. Reports of his female accomplice do not appear until the 1850s, and are clearly an invention of the unscrupulous press of the time, and an early instance of the Batman-esque bolstering of a popular cartoon-like character by giving him a sidekick. She was supposed to have been the virgin daughter of a ruined parson, first murdered and then raised from the dead by Jack (who was sometimes attributed vampiric powers).

According to legend, she would sit high above on the edges of buildings, smoking cigars and cackling as he carried out his (often sexually violent) attacks. On one occasion she swooped down, enfolding the terrified victim in her cloak, and sucking him dry of blood. This is how it was hysterically reported in the *Tooting Examiner*, anyhow. A sober analysis by the *Tooting Guardian* revealed a more prosaic cause – that the 'victim', known locally as Grouchy Dan, was a notorious drunk. He had got his hair trapped in the grate while trying to retrieve a penny from a drain and, his screams ignored by a passing public all too used to his drunken rages, he starved to death. He is buried on Tooting Common, in the duck pond. But the myth won out, of course, and when a second local tube station came to be built in SW17 the superstitious builders and engineers gave it the name that remains to this day.

ROGER WILLIAM JAMES, WORCESTER PARK

What is the origin of the word 'cottaging'?

Iwea Musube, Lagos

'Cottaging' is a lovely, evocative term, as quintessentially English and comforting as a warm pint of ale in a country public house. One thinks of the simple pleasures of a roaring log fire, and a wisp of chimney smoke hanging over the thatched roofs of an Oxfordshire village; a tabby cat lazing languidly in the afternoon sunshine of a perfect summer's day, against a hazy backdrop of foxgloves and honeysuckle and bumblebees going about their afternoon business. 'Cottaging'.

I have to be honest, though: I've never known what all that has to do with poking your old man through a 'glory hole' and being sucked down to the conkers.

CHARLES MOORELAND, NATIONAL TRUST

Not much help from old 'Conkers' Mooreland, there. He's been going into the local public toilet in Nottingham's 'slab square' for the last seven years, hoping to meet George Michael. IT'S NOT GOING TO HAPPEN, MOORELAND. Anyway, cottaging: it's something to do with the Hansel and Gretel fairy story, I think – you know, the bit where Hansel goes into the gingerbread cottage hoping to get a treat; and tricks the old witch every time by sticking a 'bone' out of the cage so she thinks he's too skinny to eat. And don't even ask what 'gingerbreading' is.

JAMES 'RANDY' JACKSON, NOTTINGHAM

T he world is safer than ever, by all scientific measures. So what are you afraid of?

Malcolm Crabs, Reading

Terrorists, paedophiles, paedophilic terrorists, MRSA, HIV, H5N1, the M52, inheritance tax, unhygienic apple-bobbing, mice laying small jellied babies in my open mouth as I sleep, Napoleon's return, fever-dreams of being repeatedly headslapped like the old man on Benny Hill, crotchless panties, glory holes and 'slack grannies'. I don't go out much.

TREVOR STOAT, BORDERS

If Stephen Hawking is so clever, how come he doesn't write *The Complete History of Time*?

Wayne Spokes, Coventry

Where would our merry band of *Old Git* readers be without the timeless idiocy of Wayne Spokes's questions? For once, however, he raises a question far more interesting, philosophically, than last month's 'If I were to sneeze and fart at the same time, would I become measurably shorter?'

Young Master Spokes's question is interesting because, of course, the young, athletic Hawking's hubris really did once extend – theoretically at least – to writing a complete history of time. Reasoning that time (as he then believed) was circular, Hawking sketched out a plan whereby all the computers in the world might be linked together and ordered to write a history of the past, present and future as it occurred – though that history could only be listened back to in full over the course of an entire second circuit through the expansion and contraction of the known universe.

At least, that was Hawking's plan until the arrival of a youthful Dr Jeremy Petting – our beloved future king, quadruple Nobel winner, male model and billionaire playboy – in Hawking's undergraduate study room looking somewhat worse for wear, claiming to have just stumbled over to say hello from 'a hell of a party in the twenty-fifth century'. According to an interview with Hawking in 1997, Petting had sat down and told an extraordinary tale, of a life spent travelling through time following a now-unknown rival, one Dr Karl Beerbohm, in what sounds like nothing so much as an unlikely cosmic episode of a *Tom and Jerry* cartoon: setting fire to Beerbohm's wig at his first wedding, genetically engineering an eighteenth-century Beerbohm forebear so that all his descendants would have no eyebrows, and such like. It is fair to say that the young Hawking had probably smoked a bit too much of the good stuff when writing his journal that night; but he has none the less always said, on record, that his now-accepted theory of time as being essentially *conical* in form, comes from his meeting with Petting. A complete history of horseshit, I say.

DON MAYWEATHER, BUCKS

All this talk of eternities spent reviewing eternities reminded me that such instances of absurd 1:1 scale undertakings are not new. In the fourteenth century, the Chinese Emperor Hu (of the Wang dynasty) ordered his chief advisor to draw up a full-scale map of his empire, as a lasting measure of his conquests. The map was, according to contemporary sources, quite exquisite: made from the finest parchment, its rich-blue seas were rendered with lapis-lazuli from Badakhstan, the grasslands a glittering carpet of Russian emeralds, while full-sized alabaster people and livestock, intricately carved, were moved around every day by foreign slaves to mirror exactly the present whereabouts of Hu's subjects. By its very nature, of course, the map could never be finished. For every new acre of map, a new acre of enemy land had to be subdued on which it could be laid; but each new conquered acre itself demanded a new acre of map to represent it.

It soon becomes clear, from tax records of the time, that Hu's subjects were increasingly ordered to stand still, since not enough slaves could be found to keep moving the heavy alabaster models around to match their movements. The effect on the Chinese economy and the well-being of its people can be easily imagined. Hu's hated map must have been one of the wonders of the world, but none of it remains; the only clues as to its fate, and that of its creator, rest in a cryptic inscription on the Emperor's magnificent tomb in Beijing:

> Here lies Hu, child of the sun,
> battered to death with an alabaster pig

HARVEY SCROTE, OTTAWA

[Ed note: Good Non-Denominational God, Penelope! What a way to go. It reminds me of a horrible prank played on me at the office medieval night last year after which I woke up with an apple in my mouth and grazed knees. Anyway: with all this talk of silly mistakes of scale, this might be a good time to bring up a favour I need to ask. You may know of that lovely statuette of 'boy and horse' that I ordered from an Italian art catalogue last month – the handsome marble figurine that I had earmarked to smarten up my desk next to the Newton's Cradle? Well, owing to a miscalculation in the ordering process – possibly attributable to me – it's arrived and it's fourteen feet tall. When you get a moment, could you 'saddle up' and get it out of reception? We're getting complaints from the Young Gits. Thanks Penelope!]

Corrections & Clarfications

Many apologies to Miss Celia Culhoon, for mistakenly printing the news of her triumphant social *début* alongside a photograph of a gibbon's arsehole (November issue). As readers will have guessed, this was merely the result of a malfunction of the picture department's ZX 81 computer, which wrongly linked Captain Featherstonehaugh's 'The Music of Africa' folder with our monthly society pages. Similarly, the image on page 56 really is that of a chimp playing a banjo, and not of handsome newborn Master Timothy Bradshaw (5lbs 2oz). If the photograph piqued your interest, however, do look out for Featherstonehaugh's jolly piece, 'Bungling Bonobos with Banjos in the Wrong Congo Jungle' in next month's issue.

Does Father Christmas exist?

Billy Braithwaite, aged ten

This question is not as ridiculous as it might at first seem. Children under the age of six make up fully 8 per cent of the British population, and the fact that they believe wholeheartedly in Santa – as opposed to a mere 7 per cent of the British population who believe wholeheartedly in God – suggests that, numerically at least, Saint Nicholas's existence should be taken very seriously indeed. I have to say, my own children – Emily, aged four, and Michael, aged three – were terribly excited to see a jolly Father Christmas 'climbing' the eaves of Janet and Ted Jamieson's house next door this year, and I for one find this new trend in festive decoration most charming. Or at least, I did; once it got to early March, I came home from work to find Ted cutting Santa's body down. The children were thrilled, until it became clear that the figure was actually a local burglar that the Jamiesons had dressed in a Santa suit and strung up in order to make an example of him. Still, the whole street plans to reconvene this coming November fifth and burn the body in a massive wicker man, so at least the kids have something to look forward to.

BRIAN MCCLOUD, SKYE

Am I alone in wondering who the hell 'Billy Braithwaite, aged ten', actually is? His age seems to change from nine to eleven and back to ten. Checking over the microfiche back issues of the *Old Git* at my local library, it becomes clear very quickly that young Master Braithwaite has been submitting childishly simple questions for the last twenty-five years; questions which, when answered, build up a broad portrait of cultural life in Britain. At once, I began to look for patterns in his questions: most are imbecilic in the extreme, but clues began to emerge. 'What is Jordan?' was a favourite, from the early 2000s, as was the somewhat puzzling query from a ten-year-old child: 'If a murder has almost certainly been committed but proof of *mens rea* remains elusive, how should one instruct the jury?' I'm sorry to say it, but matching up the questions and dates, I can only come to the conclusion that 'Billy Braithwaite' is none other than Lord Chief Justice Sir Dominic Kingston.

WENDY ALPACA, BIRMINGHAM

I went to an all-boys' school back in the 1950s and I've always wondered: why don't women fill up with water as soon as they jump in a swimming pool or have a bath?

Billy Braithwaite, aged ten

Dominic, old stick – I have to say, even though I have taught sex education at our old alma mater for many, many years, I am still baffled by this problem. Hell, I'm still fascinated by the idea of 'tights' – I mean, do women put them on before, or after, their knickers? Anyway, to answer your question, I think that's why tight swimming costumes were first invented, but I could be wrong. Tell you what, I'll write in next month as Billy Braithwaite if no one answers, yes?

TOBIAS TREACLER, ST GUFFIN'S SCHOOL FOR BOYS

If the Queen Vic in *EastEnders* is supposed to be the archetypal British pub, why does no one ever swear, talk about the football or mention *EastEnders*?

Barry Becleuch, Dumfriesshire

Fuck off, Barry, you nonce.

TERRY GRIPE, WALTHAMSTOW

Is it better to have loved and lost?

Elizabeth Beteljeuse, Hartlepool

It is, as you would be told by a million would-be poets, better that way. But of course they would say that, wondering why they're still single, standing duffle-coated by the bus stop.

Romantic tragedies abound in literature, but they are rarer in history – one exception is the case of the forgetful scholar Romanek Baflavios, a bespectacled Greek who

154

made his name by translations of Ovid that painted the Metamorphoses as a series of sexual analogies. He was fêted in academic circles and made tours of Europe to seats of learning to expound his amusing theories.

But on one of these excursions he lost his beloved wife, after having told her to stay with the luggage while he explored another platform to see if it held their train. Finding his seat, he left for Geneva without her. After he returned to London he was sure he'd forgotten something, patting his pockets and recounting his bags, before realising the magnitude of his mistake. It broke his heart and hugely aggravated his abstraction of mind – he travelled constantly for the next thirty years through the cities of Europe hoping to catch sight of her again, in the process losing his glasses, his passport, his sense of perspective and finally his marbles. This, even though the miffed missus (who had married a member of the Flemish gentry in the meantime), regularly sent him postcards with her address, each of which he would mislay before he could copy it down.

He died distraught in a Venetian asylum raving to the end about where he had lost his wife and trying desperately to remember 'Where was the last place I saw her?', the sorry mantra of anyone who's lost anything. Would he have preferred never to have loved at all, than to have loved and lost, though? Only he could have told us.

RENÉ CLIMENT, ALSACE

Is the grass really greener on the other side? How do we calculate greenness?

Graham Smite, Beiling

Amazingly, this is scientifically correct – the grass *is* greener on the other side. Or rather, as the saying should have it, the grass *appears* greener there. And it has nothing to do with chlorophyll levels – merely the shape of the grass blade as it naturally grows. Looked at from above, grass presents its wax-coated upper leaf, which protects it from heavy rain and darkens its surface slightly, therefore where one stands, looking down, it appears darker. From further away ('the other side', one imagines, of a metaphorical stream or river), however, one will see the majority of the underleaf, which is coated in no protective layer so it can absorb moisture from the air. This underside also shows brighter against sunshine and so appears greener – or, more accurately, brighter green.

BRENDA GIBSPILL, AYR

I always thought the grass was greener on the other side. Prick called Jones next door – what are the odds? – drives a Beemer, six foot four in his stockinged feet, wife with bangers you wouldn't believe, latest iPhone, pulls in £150k a year, speaks fifteen languages . . . Anyway, since he moved in, every week I've pissed in a tea tray, frozen it and posted it through his letter box ready for when he comes home; and every week I mow the word 'Twat' into his lawn in a different language. The internet is a brilliant invention. Three months into the experiment, he probably thinks life's greener on my side of the fence now.

WADE STRUMMOCK, ALDEROVER, NOTTS

[Molly – Marc here. I've had it with trying to turn the Old Git *around. Every time I send out an email to gee everyone up, every up-message podcast I send, everything gets sabotaged. I know you've been working from home because of your bad back – and it's very kind of Penelope in the* Old Git *offices to keep biking my messages over to you to be typed up – but I've come to the conclusion that it must be you who's inserting rude words, yeah? I'm sorry, Molly, but I'm going to have to let you go. Our cockjockey pondscum readers deserve more than to be insulted every time I try to tell them how pissing valued they are. Over and out, Marc.]*

If you are a Christian and hope to go to Heaven, will you spend the rest of Eternity the age you were when you died?

Margaret Spume, Clifton

Clearly, no one can give a definitive answer to this question, but the Vatican has certainly done its best over the centuries to assimilate the problem into church doctrine. A Heaven full of people exactly in the condition when they died would be somewhere between a butcher's and a bingo hall, and successive Papal bulls in the sixteenth century attempted to reassure the laity that any good Catholic could look forward to presenting himself in front of the Lord in rude health, as young or as old as they liked.

Unfortunately, this led to a rash of final deathbed confessions that were not so much humble submissions to God's will, as shopping lists for a spiritual makeover. The most famous is that of Leonardo Da Vinci, whose last words are said to have been 'I should like to fly; a full head of hair would be nice, and maybe a couple more inches ['*qualque pollice*'], you know . . .?'

Horrified, the Church withdrew the offer and drew various rhetorical veils over the mystery of Eternity, making no promises and leaving the faithful to wonder: will I come back as a glossy, firm-bellied but rather stupid teenager, or as a wiser, older version of myself with gammy knees?

RAEF ARMADA, DEPT CATHOLIC STUDIES, SHREWSBURY UNIVERSITY

It strikes me that this question raises further doubts about what state any of us might be in when we meet the Lord. I'm thinking in particular of the late Bishop of Kent, who tragically died confronting a burglar with a golf club, wearing only his wife's 'Make Poverty History' T-shirt. Presenting oneself before God with one's family jewels hanging in the breeze (and holding an utterly useless seven iron, bent to the shape of a hoody's noggin) isn't, perhaps, what the late bishop might have been praying for, for the rest of Eternity.

And what of the awful day when the roof fell in at the 1956 annual Polish Cardinals' Christmas fancy dress party? What became of Monseigneurs Wovchiechowski and Sabotka, who in a scampish festive gesture had chosen to mock God's enemies by dressing respectively as the Whore of Babylon and a cloven-hooved Satan in bright red tights? Poor Sabotka. I can't help but imagine him arriving before St Peter and saying, 'Now I know this looks bad, but I can explain . . .'

SIOBHAN O'BARNABUS, DUBLIN PUBLIC RECORDS OFFICE

Is it true that the universe is expanding outwards to infinity and that there's nothing we can do about it?

Anderson Sorbelt, Antwerp

I've looked into this since reading the question and apparently it *is* true! Either that, or at some point the contents of the universe are going to crunch together in one ghastly lump, crushing everything.

This is *exactly* the sort of thing my lying shitbag of an ex-husband Leonard would have dreamed up! The more I read the more it has all the signs of his grubby fingerprints over the whole scheme of things. It's worse than that time my sister Wendy saw him through the windows of the Big Bang nightclub groping some straw-haired strumpet when he was supposed to be at a pilates class. I am at my wit's end. Is there nothing he won't stoop to?

DEBORAH MEWS, SLOUGH

Dear Mrs Mews, I read your letter with considerable alarm and a sense of horrific revelation. For decades I have studied the various historical forces of destruction and evil. The capitalist hegemony that oppresses the large majority of all humanity, starving it of food and education; the historical certainty that all great socialist revolutions lead to even worse systems of tyranny, corruption and death; the very structure of the life form we call the virus and its destructive biological drive; the evils of organised religion and the spread of alcoholism, widespread habitual tobacco and drug abuse in the developed and developing worlds, obesity, anarchy, mental indolence and terrorism.

In all these perils of the world I have through meticulous research detected a linking DNA, the 'fingerprints', as you put it, of some overarching malevolent intelligence, united under the banner 'Immanent Unnamed Evil Studies' in my self-run department. But now the culprit is revealed, which represents a great leap forward in this important field of understanding. I will call the sign-painter tomorrow morning and return with renewed energy to my efforts to properly uncover the full crimes of this universal villain.

GRIGORAI MASP-LOTOV, DEPT OF LEONARD MEWS STUDIES,
VLADIVOSTOK UNIVERSITY

OK, my ex-wife is capable of a good practical joke when she wants, and I know she was angry that I got the sofa in the (unusually amicable) split, but having good-humouredly put up with the previous cracks, I'm afraid this is going a bit far. The *Old Git* may be my favourite magazine (the recipes page is delightfully eccentric and amusing, and the Yiddish-language crossword is a monthly challenge I relish), but that's why she attacked me through these pages, and this is now beyond a joke. The next thing I know you'll be printing my full address so this bunch of whackjobs and freak-outs can hunt me down! Please cancel my subscription and don't bother returning the money for the remaining issues.

Yours,

LEONARD MEWS, 139 APPLEYARD CRESCENT, TAMWORTH,
STAFFORDSHIRE

[Ed note: Penelope, another letter from the mysterious Clarissa. And strangest of all, it was posted last Thursday and arrived this morning! I wonder who she thinks she's writing to – have a read!]

My darling H,

I'm dreadfully sorry for the shock that the contents of this letter will bring, but my analyst claims that I must try to remember what happened. He says he is my analyst, although he looks more like a policeman. He sees me every day for the two hours when I am not under sedation. So here goes, I shall try my best before the doctor returns with his syringe, and blessed oblivion.

161

Nothing extraordinary was happening at Honey Tree Cottage that day – all was (it seems to me now) blissfully quiescent. The secret 'machine' Jeremy was building was nearing completion and he worked on it night and day. He rose early and as he went out I saw Petunia playing in the garden, chatting to her imaginary friend, lost in some game.

I returned to the weatherbeaten diary that had been engrossing me for so many weeks and months with a sense of delicious apprehension, for the tale of Daniel Dorey's haunting was about to reach its end.

It took a quarter of an hour to read the final five pages when – with a rising sense of panic – I flipped back and read them again. Apparently once upon a time a little girl, very similar to the one who had drowned in his stream, had been murdered on this very ground, her murderer executed on the same spot, and her mother, a gypsy, had cursed the grounds of the cottage. Now Daniel Dorey was convinced that the girl he had seen was a ghost, and the curse had fallen on him. He believed that he could only find release by the death of another girl and another man in the same place.

The implications of this struck me like a thunderbolt, and as I rose from my chair thinking of the strange ancient plans for a 'machine' Jeremy had found left by a previous owner, I heard a terrible whooshing noise and ran for the door. I saw an enormous conflagration overwhelming the outhouse Jeremy was working in – it was in the heart of a pulsing, rushing bonfire. I turned, dizzy, to look for Petunia and found her nowhere, nor any sign of Jeremy, who I knew must have been inside the burning building. Feeling almost out of my mind, I approached the stream and looked down. And there she was, my darling Petunia, flowers in her hand, like Waterhouse's *Ophelia* staring upward from beneath the water. Reality began to escape from me. I could feel myself turning mad. The last thing I thought I saw was a shadow, that of a tall thin man, dark-haired in a dark old-fashioned coat, his face turned away from me, running towards the woods. As he ran his body seemed to turn into powdery smoke and as he reached the trees he dissolved into nothing.

And that is all. Honey Tree Cottage was not a new lease of life but a death notice for – I can't even – dear H – they *will* let me go? They didn't think that *I* could have——

Here comes the doctor now.

Envelope stamped: 'This letter has been approved for external postage by the ward nurse on behalf of patient Clarissa Famthorpe.' Broadmoor Hospital for the Criminally Insane, Broadmoor.

Are there any taboos left?

Arturo Dominico, El Salvador

No. As wise commentators are always pointing out, we have totally exhausted the list of our civilisation's taboos. That's why we casually burn babies in the street, and open racist slurs are the stock-in-trade of the up-and-coming generation of stand-up comedians. Hence also the common acceptance and approval of the international child-sex slave trade, the opening up of borders to drugs smugglers (and the government's generous round of tax breaks to encourage the industry, now it's all legal and above board) and the *Daily Mail*'s recent 'Welcome Foreigners!' campaign to encourage immigration and integration. If only some taboos remained!

MARLEY SHELKIRK, ORKNEYS

I should say so! Perhaps British society is jaded enough to let anything slide. But on a recent trip to Saudi Arabia I found the place was intolerant to all sorts of innocuous behaviour. Desperate with thirst and cracking open my duty free litre of Bell's in a downtown marketplace, the crowd instantly exploded into uproar. A playful attempt to start a game of kiss-chase with a local beauty (well, she had beautiful *eyes*, anyway) caused a similar ruckus.

Thence to Turkey, and an interested question to the gents in the local baths about the Armenian atrocities of 1915–17, and this time I had to be airlifted by UN peacekeepers once the embassy was surrounded. I thought I was home and dry in the south of France, but politely requesting a deodorant in a supermarket, had to dive into the Med ahead of an angry mob. No taboos, indeed. How exhausting!

N. COGNITO, BARCELONA

[Me again, Penny! Nearly home! What a year of travels, what a year. The above doesn't quite cover the scrapes I got into in the Middle East. I really must read a newspaper more often, you know, things change so fast. There was I reliving the glory

164

days of WWII, roaring across the desert in a stolen Jeep and looking for signs to Persia. Was hoping to relive that jaunt with old Paddy Whipsthistle and visit the Marsh Arabs, but they were gone, gone, gone. Where the frail ecology of the Arabian marshlands had shimmered stood a remarkably well-stocked 7-Eleven, in which after recovering from my shock with a few double-shot lattes from their machine, I found the latest Old Git and caught up on the news. GOOD WORK sabotaging the Young Git, Penny! You're a star! Take their pounding music and their modish, lazy copywriting and stick it in the new editor's arsehole! I intend to be back in six weeks and to rescue you from this horror, but before then I need a little help. Arrived in Tangier with a fearful recurrence of the old back pain (carrying three suitcases laden with trinkets) and got into an ungodly misunderstanding when a local offered me 'a boy to unburden my load'. Phrasebook (which I see was originally compiled by Joe Orton) let me down more than somewhat, and while my cell has a sensational view out over the Kasbah's spectacular sunsets, it also looks down on the prison gallows. I'm smuggling this out via Armal, the sympathetic prison guard and long-time OG reader – Penny, telegram Reggy Braithwaite at the Foreign Office! Please! My life depends on you! Your ex-editor. XX]

There certainly seemed to be taboos left for one Edgar Algernon Montescue, an unsuccessful entrepreneur who attempted to establish a chain of peep-show houses in Soho in the 1970s.

I had been to Eton with Edgar in the 1950s, where even by the priggish standards of those days he showed himself to have had an unnatural, unusually blinkered and sheltered upbringing with two maiden aunts near Whitby. Public school brings out perversion in the best of boys, though (and if it isn't there to be brought out, it introduces it with a vengeance), and Edgar showed a predilection for prurient publications and naughty postcards. At least we *thought* that was the reason his face went bright pink and his voice squeaked if you caught him reading under the covers. One day after he had been sent to the infirmary we other boys plundered his stash, eager to supplement our own, and discovered they were nothing more than Edwardian fashion magazines, showing paintings of well-dressed ladies posing on Brighton pier, or leaning their parasols against the rail at Ascot. Baffled at this, and half-fearing we had unearthed a perversion weirder than our own (which went no further than casual buggery) we left them well alone.

When Montescue's name came to the public's attention twenty years later, I paid close attention. He had opened two 'parlours' south of Oxford Street that would 'seek', as Edgar put it in one of the many interviews at the time, 'to satisfy the secret needs of gentlemen in our hitherto repressed society'.

In the second month of his flagship store's opening, fearful that I might soon be deprived of what was bound to be a brilliant dinner party tale by the business's imminent collapse, I attended an afternoon 'peep show' at Lady Margaret's Special Boutique. Scurrying inside I was greeted by a clearly bored blonde in a frilly maid's costume that covered every inch of her skin except her face and the top centimetre of neck. She showed me to my table, where I was provided with refreshments which were of a very high price and decidedly low quality, as is the norm with such establishments (I am informed). I was delighted to find that the interior had been decked out like a saloon bar circa 1910, and to notice that the waitresses' costumes were intended to replicate those of a Lyons Tea Shop of the same era.

When the show itself started, a pretty girl in a get-up that Mary Poppins would have found stifling marched haughtily on to the stage. Instead of taking her clothes off she behaved exactly like one of those Edwardian models I had briefly glimpsed decades before, primly posing with her parasol and pretending to spy a far-off acquaintance before very slowly taking off one of her gloves. At the revelation of her naked hand there were gasps and spontaneous applause from several members of the audience – several others rushed to the gents in evident distraction – and I can't deny that it was a small personal revelation. In the remainder of the act the talented girl performed several acts of dainty and miniature exhibitionism, each of which had the impact of a thunderclap on the assembled viewers, culminating in a manoeuvre where she dropped her purse and bent to retrieve it, the hem of her dress rising to expose a small triangle of flesh above the top of her ankle. I could take no more. Flicking up the collar of my coat and pulling down my hat, I sheepishly retreated around the corner back to Barney's Sex Shop. I never heard of Edgar again.

BARNEY 'FATFACE' SMITH, CENTRAL LONDON

If I commit a crime on an aeroplane, does it mean that no country has jurisdiction over me? And does anyone know a good lawyer?

Gaston LeFange, Ontario

You make an interesting point, Mr LeFange. Here at the Los Angeles Police Department, we have a lot of experience of just this problem. Rich teenagers from Beverly Hills, tired of waiting for their twenty-first birthday, have taken to boozing on their parents' helicopters hovering just off the Malibu coast. And one asshole I tried to put in jail for underage drinking – little c*cksucker called Bud Chipman – used to jump while swigging from the bottle, every time I attempted to apprehend him! He successfully argued in court that I couldn't nab him in mid-air, because he was out of LAPD jurisdiction. So to answer your question: yes, you probably would get away with it. A word of caution, though, Mr LeFange; it's hard to jump if someone cuffs you to a fire hydrant, beats you about the face and neck with a nightstick and photographs you with a bottle of bourbon stuck to your mouth. Hey Chipman – here's lookin' at you, you little c*cksucker!

OFFICER BRAD FUDMAN, LAPD

I f a penalty shoot-out is indecisive after the whole team have taken one, how do you decide a knock-out match?

Genny Jeras, London

This was only properly considered ten years ago when, to the alarm of FIFA, the outcome of the Ultra Cup (which was decided between the winners of the Super Cup, the European Cup Winners' Cup, the European Cup and the runners-up of the Cup Winners' Cup – that is, until it was abolished in 2001 for being ridiculous) hung in the balance after nine penalties apiece. At that point Inter Milan's Zeno Bambini caused a storm by striking the ball so hard at the goalkeeper that it bounced off his forehead, hit a small ballboy on the touchline and spun into the far corner of the net. In the legal wrangles that followed, a new rules commissar was appointed to ensure that all referees would know how to proceed in *all possible outcomes* at such a crucial juncture.

The man appointed for the task, Swede Ogder Streiersand, came up with a sixty-four-page document that was hailed as a masterpiece in the grand tradition of mindless European bureaucratic doodling. No one could read this dense statistic-based treatise to the end, which is just as well, because by midway through compiling it his mind, bent to breaking point with all the reading and analysis, seemed to snap. First he proposed coin tosses (up to a hundred of these), hundred-yard sprints, hand-standing contests and a game of snap to be played with a FIFA-approved sealed deck of cards to be kept in a safe guarded by a fifth official.

Presuming all these came out equal, he concluded that the very laws of chance themselves were against an outcome, and that logic should be thrown out of the window: a custard pie fight next (only oven gloves and basic ingredients would be provided), followed by an on-pitch game of hide and seek, and then six weeks of training by professional opera singers to conclude with each side putting on a production of *HMS Pinafore*. This would be judged by a panel of unqualified dentists plucked from a variety of little-known Pacific islands, and the captain of the winning side would be obliged to appear at that year's Royal Variety Performance, singing 'I Am the Very Model of a Modern Major General'.

He resigned his commission shortly after the document's publication, when he was offered a job on the planning committee for Heathrow Terminal 5.

CLARE SELSIUS, HONOLULU

Corrections & Clarfications

We would like to apologise for printing Donald Sommersby's letter (May issue) announcing his discovery of Hergé's lost overtly racist Tin Tin book, *Tin Tin and the White Pointy Hat*. As Matthew Spink pointed out in a letter to the editor, *Tin Tin and the White Pointy Hat* is clearly a fake, massively substandard to Hergé's real masterworks. The editorial team here at the *Old Git* are all avid fans of Hergé's books and would like to draw a line under the debate. Only a pantywaist liberal would find anything wrong in the old-gold magic to be found in *Cigars of the Pharaoh*, *Tin Tin in the Congo* and *The Adventures of Tin Tin: The Quest for Lebensraum*.

New Scotland Yard

Dear Penelope,

I hoped to catch you in person, but I was called away on another case. My name is Inspector Rambull of Scotland Yard. I am gravely sorry that you have come back to discover everyone in your office has been murdered. Yes, after the deaths of your milkman and the staff in the upstairs and downstairs office, we now truly believe that we have a serial killer on our hands, a terrifying psychopath to rival or exceed the horrors brought about not far from your offices by Jack the Ripper one hundred and thirty years ago. Unlike that man, however, this villain will be caught. Please don't be afraid on that count.

Of course life must go on, so I have allowed you access back into your office. You must – you *must* – ignore the chalk outlines of all your dead colleagues over the floors, against the walls and one, inconveniently for you, on the toilet. But I'm sure you can use the loos in either the upstairs or the downstairs offices. They won't be needing it any more after they were knocked off in just such a bloodcurdling fashion. As the sole survivor you will be under twenty-four-hour surveillance, so feel no fear.

So that you know, the evidence as it presented itself to us offered no leads. Nothing connects the victims except the *Old Git* and its passionately deranged correspondents. Reading through all the columns of your corrections and clarificiations

171

(I've never got that word right) column, certain suspects emerged. First we raided the home of one Simon Sayers in County Durham, but all we found was a simpleton doodling around with crayons and paper in his garage. We questioned him for three hours, but when he still showed no sign of even understanding what we were talking about, let alone denying his involvement, we gave up. Instead we tore across the country to apprehend the next suspect, a man noted for his aggression, hostility, ignorance and history of violence.

General Smythington-Smythe's house was silent, and his frail and utterly drunken wife, apparently trapped in a deep armchair, proved incapable of determining his whereabouts or anything else at all, even if she had wished to, and had been cruelly made up to look like a black and white minstrel. The armed response unit swarmed into the garden to seek out sheds or bolt holes where he may have planned his atrocities. That was where they found the old man trapped in a prize melon, where he claimed to have tripped and fallen. But there is no guessing the perversion of some characters. His utter bewilderment at being presented with an arrest warrant, his childlike tears (and an hour's obliterating search of his house) proved his innocence. (We even briefly suspected a man called Leonard Mews due to the crimes piled on his head by his wife Deborah, but it turned out he was just an average cheating scumbag who had been found thrashing about with his mistress in the local woods, so we beat the crap out of him anyway.)

Then, on the journey back to Scotland Yard, in a frustrated scouring of the archives, the penny (if you'll excuse the pun) dropped. Not that the killer was you – I don't mean that. But a man who tracked your every move and obsessed about everyone you had contact with, with a murderous passion. His first letter arrived in your first week on the journal. His every communication is rent with psychotic simplicity and schizoid delusion, and (the key to every sociopath) absolute humourlessness. So now we know, murder has been given a new flavour, painted a new colour, and it is called:

Plum.

No Plum is listed in Plumstead. Yet a hundred constables scour the streets as you read this. They know what they're looking for: a loner who seems normal to his neighbours, who has a menial or meaningless office job, and a collection of brightly coloured jumpers and offensive ties. We'll have him in a matter of hours. You have this as my word.

Detective Inspector Rambull,
New Scotland Yard

Is there any difference between blogging and what I would call 'typing'?

Sarah Fellingham, Edinburgh

Indeed there is not, Sarah. Just as Jack Kerouac battered away on an old typewriter for three days and called *On the Road* a book, it seems that these days anyone can tap away at their keyboards about the price of milk and their latest haircut, and call it 'literature'. Who was it who said that, given a few thousand years, a chimpanzee could randomly hit typewriter keys and come up with the complete works of Shakespeare? Well, it turns out they're probably right: after an estimated 400 million halfwits merrily blogging away every day for the last five years, my researchers discovered that the first two lines of Wordsworth's *Prelude* had been miraculously produced by one Wayne Spokes, aged fifteen, of Coventry:

> '. . . WELL nang! She is bare BUTTERS lol but shez got massive bangers I still would but O! There is a blessing in this gentle breeze, a visitant that, while it fans my cheek, doth seem half conscious of the joy it brings to me, long sojourned from watching City at the weekend I fooking LOVE IT rolling-on-floor-laughing-my-arse-off!!!!!'

LIZ GOUGH, KING'S CROSS

Dear Penny, like all your readers I'm terribly sorry for your loss, but pleased and proud that you are keeping up the tradition and not letting the *Old Git* die. I've always wanted to know: if God is supposed to have created Heaven, Earth, the Universe and every single object and creature within it, how can religious people believe in a personal god who understands them and empathises with them personally, when his intellect must be so much vaster than ours as to be comparable to that of a human regarding an amoeba through a microscope? Have they really thought it through? Can they really believe it?

Uriah Hobee, Tallinn

Uriah, no one really believes in this any more. Except, as you posit, those who don't think about it much. Most priests of any denomination I have known, after their years of theological training, understand the idea to be quite frivolous, and that God is at his best when taken just as an idea and nothing else. In fact, I have lived as (I hope) a relatively good Christian for the last forty years without considering God to be real for a second except at times of terrible emotional crisis, when I have needed to.

But a certain young man I met overcame this and made his very own personal God. Cuby Romaine was his name, a good and ferociously bright boy who, rejecting his parents' Catholic god, imbued the same values he had learned (and which he knew to be basically good, positive ones) in his favourite sock, which he called Captain Lawrence.

He prayed to Captain Lawrence at the beginning and end of each day, and followed his ever-increasing list of laws to the last letter. What's more, he enjoyed a full and complete love with his very own God much like that of other believers but more personal. It made him feel chosen and act like a saint, helped by the fact that his intellectually inferior parents feared him, and were very distant. And if the word of god handed down to Cuby became more and more personal and idiosyncratic ('Thou shalt replace thy toothbrush because it's so splayed now it can't be cleaning your teeth properly and a Transformers one can't be appropriate any more now you're thirteen' ran the 487th Commandment), it was because it was his own personal god – so why not?

Once Cuby, who was a perceptive, disciplined and courteous English literature pupil of mine, reached adolescence, he began to see cracks even in his own bespoke religion. He saw that adults are driven by contrary and complex forces that cannot (and should not always be forced to) be resolved, only understood. He met a nice local girl called Meg, and Captain Lawrence's stand on sex before marriage, which had been such an easy moral portcullis when he was a child, seemed all of a sudden woefully out of date and simplistic.

Once a god is distrusted on a single issue, he must be partly undermined on *all* of them. And then how much more that counts for a personal god. I encouraged Cuby's writing and saw that as he grew into his mid- and late-teens his schooltime genuflections to Captain Lawrence (he had always pretended not to notice the ridicule he received for these) became infrequent and then forgotten.

At eighteen the precocious boy had an article placed with the *New Yorker*, and invited Meg and me around for dinner. As I stood outside waiting for the bell to be answered, I saw a familiar sock on the top of the trash in the garbage can a few yards away. Unaccountably,

I felt a pang of pity – not for Cuby who had grown beyond it, but for Captain Lawrence, inanimate, unworshipped, just a sock. I won't mention it at Cuby's Pulitzer Prize ceremony next month, and neither will he, but I think both of us are happy that Captain Lawrence once existed.

LAURA TONES-FENKZE, SCRANTON, N.J.

Corrections & Clarfications

We should like to apologise for the computer error that led to an embarrassing misprinted headline in our May Issue, 'Jeremy Clarkson Blows Pigs'. That the phrase 'Jeremy Clarkson Blows Pigs' subsequently appeared in every line of every article within that issue in place of the word 'and' is even more unfortunate, and we should like to make it clear that we bear Mr Clarkson no ill-will. 'Jeremy Clarkson Blows Pigs' is a lie, pure and simple, and we would like to make clear that Mr Clarkson is a paragon of virtue in the presence of all livestock, whether ovine, porcine or equine, and furthermore constitutes no risk whatsoever to either working animals or domestic pets.

[Penny, it's me, the old Editor! Sorry for crashing through the window like Bruce Willis, but I just had to settle upon a suitably filmic ending to the adventures of the last few months. No, stop typing up what I say, turn around and give me a kiss, you lovely thing! I mean it, no, look, put the typewriter down, I can't get my arms around you . . . Yes, yes,

of course you can ask Molly to take over writing all of this down; always the completist, Penny! That's why I love you. There now, oh my darling Penny, fire of my loins, my light, my life, my slip-slop, mwah mwah, MOLLY!, you don't have to write out sound-effects of our passionate embrace, dear girl! Yes, I know I seem out of breath; I have come straight from Scotland Yard, where that blackguard Plum is finally under lock and key. Aided by the sturdy Inspector Rambull, I pursued Plum across the city in a fearsomely exciting chase of which Hitchcock himself would have been proud: holding on to Nelson's privates for dear life at the top of his column in Trafalgar Square; snaking through the opium dens of Soho and then, hours later, past the guns of HMS Belfast, Plum taunting me in a grim approximation of Cher in the music video for 'If I Could Turn Back Time', then to Tower Bridge itself, where I was forced to leap across the opening leaves of the road bridge in order to bring Plum to ground – as classic a rugby football tackle as you will ever see, girls. Naturally, Plum would not give up without a fight – after Rambull had read him his rights, as he was dragged away he could be heard asking to hear his 'lefts' – but his reign of terror is at an end. Oh Penny, will you marry me? Say that you will!]